BEASTS
AND BEAUTIES

CINEMA'S GOLDEN AGE OF GORILLA MEN, KILLER APES & MISSING LINKS

AN ILLUSTRATED FILMOGRAPHY 1908–1949

BEASTS AND BEAUTIES
ISBN 978-1-84068-693-7
Edited by G.H. Janus
All material copyright © The Nocturne Group 2022
This edition copyright © Fabbrica Sodoma 2022
All world rights reserved
Published in the USA by Deicide Press 2023
With special thanks to Black Gas Entertainment
Design: Broken Fang Cryptography

BEASTS
AND BEAUTIES

FOREWORD

A major source of inspiration for early film-makers was provided by the often grotesque mystery-horror tales of Edgar Allan Poe, notably "The Murders In The Rue Morgue" (1841), not only a prototype of the modern detective story but also the debut of another vivid cultural trope, the killer ape – in Poe's tale, a trained orang-utan that slashes the throats of its female human victims to the bloody bone. Usually portrayed by actors in costume or heavy prosthetics, early cinema's killer apes were soon joined by rampaging gorillas – either jungle-wild, circus-tamed or trained to serve wicked masters – and even a rising crop of ape-human hybrids, either evolutionary "missing links" or creatures spawned by medical experimentation and radical surgeries. While the first examples of these engineered anomalies tended to be the subject of absurdist comedies[1], later films such as **Balaoo** (1913) or **Go And Get It** (1920) would posit them as murderous haunters of the shadows.

FREMIET, *GORILLE ENLEVANT UNE FEMME.*

Another key inspiration for this body of cinema was the thinly-veiled racist trope of gorillas as abductors and ravishers of white human females, a fear which arose from early European expeditions into Africa and which was first coherently expressed in Emmanuel Fremiet's famous sculptural work *Gorille Enlevant Une Femme* ("Gorilla Abducting A Woman", 1887).[2] Found in a range of silent films, this idea found its apex expression in RKO's **King Kong** (1932) – with Fay Wray as the blonde snatched away by a giant gorilla – while its unspoken logical conclusion, a grotesque miscegenation not of races, but of species, was shown in the infamous **Ingagi** (1931). In **Ingagi**, Charles Gemora – by that time number one among the numerous gorilla impersonators in Hollywood – portrays an alpha primate who rapes and impregnates human natives[3].

Hollywood's delinquent gorilla men, seen in feature films, shorts and serials alike, persisted into the 1940s and only began to slow with the mass advent of colour cinema, making the period 1913 -1949 the golden age of beasts and beauties. This book documents that period not only with informative texts but also with a stunning array of film stills, many culled from the darkest depths of cine-archives and never published before.

Acknowledgement

All text and graphic works in this book were selected, collated and edited under license from **Shadows In A Phantom Eye**, the ongoing multi-volume global film history from The Nocturne Group which is already, in my opinion, proving to be among the best of its kind ever published. The history of gorilla-men, killer apes and missing links is just one of the hundreds of intertwining threads contained in this seminal series.

–G.H. Janus, 2022

ILLUSTRATION FOR "THE MURDERS IN THE RUE MORGUE" BY DANIEL URRABIETA Y VIERGE, 1870 (*OPPOSITE PAGE*).

1. The cinema of monkey-human hybrids began in comedies such as **Le Sérum Du Singe** (Gaumont, 1908, released in the US as **The Doctor's Experiment**), in which humans revert to simian behaviour after being injected with monkey-gland serum.

Other examples include Pathé's **L'Homme-Singe** (1909, released in the US as **The Man Monkey**), which involved a biologist opening up the skulls of a monkey and a human cretin (played by André Deed) to compare their brains; when the cretin's brain is devoured by a cat, the doctor gives him the monkey's, resulting in a gibbering rampage and scenes in a lunatic asylum; Pathé's Italian-made **Les Singeries Du Signor Ravioli** ("Mr. Ravioli's Monkey Tricks", 1909) was a vulgar treatment of a similar theme. Also from Italy was Ambrosio's 1911 production **La Scimmia Di Robinet** ("Robinet's Monkey"), in which Robinet (Marcel Fabre) wins a belligerent simian in a lottery. The beast – played by a man in a monkey-suit – proceeds to run amok, destroying everything in its path, and forcing Robinet to finally shoot it dead. Unfortunately, in his haste to obliterate the monkey, Robinet also kills his wife and mother-in-law; as the film ends he ruefully blows his own brains out, adding a fourth corpse to the pile. Extreme surgical procedures and grafting were at the core of Éclair's 1911 contribution to this absurdist genre, **M. Le Dr. Charley Est Un Grand Chirurgien** ("Dr. Charley Is A Great Surgeon"). First, the doctor cuts out a patient's stomach, washes it and hangs it out to dry; then, the man's stomach is devoured by a hungry dog; and finally, the doctor replaces it with the stomach of a monkey, resulting in the usual simian antics. The culminatory work of these monkey-farces was perhaps Pathé's **Le Singe Du Professeur Maboul** ("Professor Maboul's Monkey", 1914), a reprise of their earlier **L'Homme-Singe**. Like most tropes in early cinema, doctor-and-monkey antics can be traced back to Georges Méliès, who made **Le Savant Et Le Chimpanzé** ("The Scientist And The Chimp") in 1900, featuring one of the first actor-in-monkey-costume turns. The inspiration for some of these "ape-man" films may have come from the discoveries, in 1908 at La Chapelle-aux-Saints and in 1909 at La Ferrassie, of the most complete skeleton and skull of Neanderthal Man, popularly pictured as the "missing link" between primates and humans. However, in many of the films the victims only resemble simians in behaviour, not appearance.

2. Fears vividly displayed in a notable cinematic outburst in the early 1920s from Germany, where defeat in WWI was followed by an equally unpalatable reality – the occupation of the Rhineland by French troops, many of whom were *Tirailleurs Sénégalais* ("Senegalese Sharpshooters"), African recruits from Senegal and other countries (as seen in the 1917 French army documentary **Tirailleurs Sénégalais En Alsace**). This was perceived as an unbearable humiliation by German right-wingers, who reacted by instigating a racist backlash aimed at the French and, in particular, their negro soldiers. Starting in 1919, this propaganda painted the African troops as savage apes who roamed free in packs across Germany, raping, impregnating, infecting and murdering white women in a series of savage assaults; the image of a drooling, gorilla-like creature in a French army uniform stripping away a German girl's clothes became the prime motif of the movement, which became known as *Schwarze Schmach* – the black shame, or disgrace. Leaflets, postcards, posters, plays, badges and even novels bearing this atrocity tableau were widely disseminated; and in 1920, one of the campaign's most virulent proponents, Heinrich Distler, formed the *Deutsche Notbund gegen die Schwarze Schmach* ("German Emergency League against Black Shame"), a radical organization who pursued their agenda with an almost paramilitary efficiency and zeal. Distler was apparently an aspiring film-writer whose interest lay in quasi-pornographic exploitation cinema as a vehicle for stirring outrage, and in 1921 this blueprint would be realised. Carl Boese, who in 1920 had co-directed the horror-fantasy classic **Der Golem, Wie Er In Die Welt Kam**, followed it with a different kind of monster film, **Die Schwarze Schmach**, a cinematic realisation of Distler's racist propaganda in which a gang of rampaging Senegalese soldiers are shown attacking a young German couple, raping the woman and infecting her with venereal disease. This assault was clearly depicted on the film's sensational and provocative poster campaign. Originally designated for adults only, the film was a great success, but after a second censorship review was officially banned in August 1921 – although it reportedly continued to play in many local picture-houses. Soon after the release of **Die Schwarze Schmach**, Europa-Film of Berlin issued their own black shame tract, **Die Schwarze Pest** ("The Black Plague"), another grotesque rape-phantasy which was duly banned by the censor. Despite this prohibition, the phenomenal spectre of *Schwarze Schmach* could not be exorcised;

as a manifestation of the German craving for "racial purity", it underpinned the Aryan ideology which would allow Adolf Hitler to sweep into power during the following decade. (When the Nazis invaded France in 1940, thousands of Senegalese were among the first to be killed by vengeful firing-squad.) In cinematic terms, its imagery of bestial negroes violating white-skinned blondes clearly anticipated **King Kong,** whose monstrous ape was ultimately another cipher for the African male and his threat of defilement, disease and miscegeny. Certain German "jungle" films from around 1920, such as Fritz Bernhardt's **Darwin,** carried similar images, but it remains unclear whether this was done with explicit reference to *Schwarze Schmach* – although the growing prevalence of such iconography, also found in photographs produced at Studio Manassé in Vienna, for example, indicates a distinct Teutonic cultural trope which by the mid-1920s was fully and firmly established.

3. So popular was Gemora's gorilla act that he even appeared in staged supplementary sequences shot for the first sound jungle documentary, **Africa Speaks** (1930). However, although Gemora can be seen on posters and in promotional stills for the film, his scenes were apparently not included in the final cut.

PRELUDE: FORMING A CINEMATIC MYTHOLOGY 1908–1926

SHERLOCK HOLMES IN THE GREAT MURDER MYSTERY

(Crescent Films, 1908: USA)

Actually the first-known film version of "The Murders In The Rue Morgue", Edgar Allan Poe's mystery-horror tale about a homicidal, razor-wielding ape, substituting Arthur Conan Doyle's fashionable detective Holmes for Dupin, the French sleuth of the original. Holmes solves this bizarre and bloody crime after a trance-like meditation session, apparently. Éclair American's **The Raven** (1912), inspired by Poe's signature poem, features macabre imagery taken from "The Murders In The Rue Morgue" as well as other tales including "The Gold Bug", "The Black Cat", "The Pit And The Pendulum", "A Descent Into The Maelstrom", and "The Premature Burial". Poe himself is depicted in the film as a haunted figure. The next known film adaptations of "The Murders In The Rue Morgue" were produced in 1914; Sol Rosenberg's **The Murders In The Rue Morgue** was an American production from Paragon Photo Plays, while the German film **Das Geheimnis Des Affen** ("The Ape Mystery") was directed by Georg Jacoby, and produced by Literaria-Film of Berlin, a company set up by Pathé Frères and Duskes. Vitaskop's 1914 *krimi* **Die Braune Bestie** ("The Brown Beast"), an ape-murder-mystery, was also reportedly inspired by Poe's story. It was one in a series of sensational cine-pulps directed for the company by Harry Piel, commencing in 1912 with the "yellow peril" nightmare **Schwarzes Blut** ("Black Blood" – released in the USA as **The Hindu Nemesis**), in which an evil, hooded Asian terrorizes Germany in a rampage of kidnapping, poisoning, theft and violence. Completing a trio of German "Rue Morgue" adaptations was Felix Basch's **Fliegende Schatten** ("Fleeting Shadows", 1916), with Max Landa as the detective Dupin. Hypnotism was at the centre of **Crime And The Penalty** (1916), from British producer Martin; in this watered-down variation on the theme of "The Murders In The Rue Morgue", a scientist hypnotizes a laboratory chimpanzee to kidnap and strangle. The most bizarre film from the small outpouring of British pulp horror during this period may have been New Agency's **A Cry In The Night** (1915), directed by Ernest G. Batley, in which another deranged scientist kills by means of a monstrous creature, in this case a "winged gorilla" known as the Thing. The Thing was played by James Russell, a former member of the Fred Karno theatrical troupe which had also included future Hollywood stars Charlie Chaplin and Stan Laurel. A different kind of monster was seen in Thanhouser's **The Miser's Reversion** (1914), in which an old skinflint dreams that he overdoses on a youth elixir and regresses to a primordial, semi-simian form, making this a notable early missing link depiction.

DAS GEHEIMNIS DES AFFEN - FILM POSTER SHOWING POE'S RAZOR-WIELDING APE (*OPPOSITE*).

Le AVVENTURE STRAORDINARISSIME DI SATURNO FARANDOLA
("The Most Extraordinary Adventures Of Saturnino Farandola"; Marcel Fernández
Peréz, 1913: Italy)
Created by Peréz (also known as Marcel Fabre and comic screen persona Robinet)
with uncredited help from Luigi Maggi, **Le Avventure Straordinarissime Di Saturnino
Farandola** is a 4-part fantasy based on Albert Robida's 1879 novel *Viaggi
Straordinarissimi Di Saturnino Farandola*. With influences ranging from Georges
Méliès and Jules Verne to the Bible, Fabre's 3660-metre film was among the most
unusual and ambitious works of Italian cinema to that date. In the first episode,
L'Isola Delle Scimmie ("Monkey Island"), a ship-wrecked boy named Saturnino is
raised by monkeys, who ultimately abandon him. Leaving the island, Saturnino
begins a series of wild adventures which involve defeating pirates, becoming a sea-
captain, and marrying a native-girl named Misora; Misora is devoured by a whale,
which is captured and held in an aquarium. When the aquarium refuses to eviscerate
the whale and free Misora, Saturnino declares war and returns with a liberating army

of monkey warriors. In the subsequent episodes – *Alla Ricerca Dell'Elefante Bianco* ("In Search Of The White Elephant"), *La Regina Dei Makalolos* ("The Queen Of Makalos"), and *Farandola Contro Fileas-Fogg* ("Farandola Versus Fileas-Fogg") – Saturnino and Misora travel to Siam, Africa and America, encountering savage tribespeople, man-eating animals and, finally, a civil war fought with futuristic balloon battles, chloroform bombs, and "pneumatic vacuums". Peréz/Fabre relocated to America in 1915, making a series of comedies for various independent companies (including Vim, where he played Bungles opposite fat man Babe Hardy) until, in 1923, his leg had to be amputated – some say due to cancer, some say after he contracted septicaemia following a fall. He died a few years later.

1. The four parts were released in the USA individually by Warners, as a serial, under the titles **Zingo The Son Of The Sea**, **Zingo And The White Elephant**, **Zingo's War In The Clouds**, and **Zingo In Africa** (all 1914).

BALAOO
(Victorin-Hippolyte Jasset, 1913: France)
Based on the eponymous novella by Gaston Leroux,[1] this is one of the very first serious "ape-man" or "missing link" movies, a variant on the theme of metamorphic horror. Balaoo is an ape turned nearly human by a scientist; he has human thoughts and emotions, but the strength of a jungle killer. Known in English as **Balaoo The Demon Baboon**, the film runs for around twenty-four minutes. The story was reimagined as both **The Wizard** (1927, featuring a hideous facial graft) and **Dr. Renault's Secret** (1942). As an example of non-comic ape-human hybrid cinema, **Balaoo** was preceded by Powers Picture Plays' **The Haunted Island** (1911), in which a ship-wrecked couple are stalked by a mysterious man-monkey creature, and followed by works such as **Homo** (1915), a sinister man-ape transformation film from Italy's Savoia, also known as **La Scimmia Umana** ("The Human Ape") and **La Scimmia Vendicatrice** ("The Avenging Ape"). A more comedic entry was the Danish production **Abemennesket** ("Apeman", 1917), with an actor in a pantomime chimp costume.

1. Jasset's film was not actually the first film inspired by Leroux's *Balaoo*, which was first published in 1911 as a serial in *Le Matin* – in 1912 Abel Gance made the parodic **Il Y A Des Pieds Au Plafond** ("There Are Feet On the Ceiling"), which was never widely released due to allegations of copyright infringement (*Il Y A Des Pas Au Plafond!* – "There Are Footsteps On The Ceiling!" – was the title given to the first part of a 2-volume edition of *Balaoo* published by Tallandier in 1912).

ABEMENNESKET – PRODUCTION PHOTOGRAPH (*RIGHT*).
BALAOO – PRODUCTION PHOTOGRAPH (*OVERLEAF*).

LUCILLE LOVE: THE GIRL OF MYSTERY

(Francis Ford, 1914: USA)

One of several gynocentric action-jeopardy serials from 1914, Universal's **Lucille Love: The Girl Of Mystery** starred Grace Cunard, who became known briefly as the "Serial Queen". **Lucille Love** began as a mere 2-reel adventure, but was hastily expanded into a 15-chapter serial by Universal to cash in on the success of Pathé's girl-driven ventures in the format.[1] The chapters were untitled. Among the serial's most memorable sequences was an episode in which Lucille, acclaimed as white goddess by a savage jungle tribe, plunges into a subterranean world inhabited by demi-human ape-creatures. **Lucille Love** was later cited as a formative influence by Spanish director Luis Buñuel, who dedicated his unpublished text *Lucille Y Sus Tres Peces* ("Lucille And Her Three Fish", 1925) to the Love character.

1. Gorilla menace featured in other serials of the decade, notably **The Perils Of Pauline** (1914) and **The Red Ace** (1917). And Duke Worne's pulp classic **The Trail Of The Octopus** (1919) featured deformed actor John George as Borno, an "ape man".

The DINOSAUR AND THE MISSING LINK
(Willis O'Brien, 1915: USA)

A pioneering stop-motion animation from O'Brien, initiating the techniques displayed at maturity in his later work on **The Lost World** and **King Kong**; this 5-minute film features a dinosaur, cavemen, and an ape-like creature. This was probably the first ever stop-motion dinosaur movie – the first proper dinosaur cartoon animation was Winsor McKay's **Gertie The Dinosaur** in 1914, and fake or mechanical dinosaurs featured in such films as **Brute Force** (1914). O'Brien followed up with more short animation works including **R.F.D. 10,000 B.C.** (1916), **Prehistoric Poultry** (1916) and **The Ghost Of Slumber Mountain** (1918), which staged a dream vision of a prehistoric valley inhabited by dinosaurs and pterosaurs.

NÄCHTE DES GRAUENS
("Nights Of Terror"; Arthur Robison, 1916: Germany)

Robison's prototypical *gruselkrimi* ("weird crime thriller") is said to involve a deranged artist whose sexual jealousy leads him to don an ape-costume in order to commit a series of brutal murders. The film starred and was produced by actress Lu Synd, whose next production, **Die Frau Mit Den Zwei Seelen** ("The Woman With Two Souls", 1916) – a weird nocturne concerning a somnambulist with the power to foresee future events – was again scripted by Robison.

The National Film Corp. of America presents
TARZAN of the APES

A "First National" Attraction

TARZAN OF THE APES - PRODUCTION PHOTOGRAPH.

TARZAN OF THE APES
(Scott Sidney, 1917: USA)

The first legitimate film adaptation of Edgar Rice Burroughs' 1912 fantasy novel of a man reared by apes is perhaps the most faithful to its source (although it covers only the first part of the story). The boy Tarzan appears nude (with exposed genitals), and the breasts and buttocks of African natives (actually local blacks scooped up from skid row) are also briefly shown. The 10-reel film, released in early 1918, is also said to include an early example of "animal snuff", retaining footage of the killing of an ageing circus lion stabbed to death during production. The film was recorded in both Los Angeles and the swamps of Louisiana, and features one of the wildest of all Hollywood gorilla costumes. The "monkey folk" who raised Tarzan are also played by actors in animal-suits. Tarzan was played by Elmo Lincoln, although only because original choice Stellan Windrow was called up for active service halfway through shooting (his tree-swinging sequences are still in the film, uncredited); Lincoln played the role two more times – in **The Romance Of Tarzan** (1918), based on the second part of Burroughs' original novel, and **The Adventures Of Tarzan** (1921), a 15-chapter serial from Louis Weiss part-based on the novel *Tarzan And The Jewels Of Opar* (1916)[1]. Several more silent Tarzan films and serials followed **Tarzan Of The Apes**; Harry Revier's 15-chapter 1920 serial, **Son Of Tarzan** (based on Burroughs' eponymous 1914 novel), features some truly grotesque ape costumes and make-up, plus several nude and bare-breasted scenes with both "natives" and actress Manilla Martan,[2] while Revier's **The Revenge Of Tarzan** (originally known as **Return Of Tarzan**, 1920, based on the second Tarzan novel) is perhaps best-known for a publicity stunt pulled by legendary press agent Harry Reichenbach, who shipped a live jungle lion into a Manhattan hotel.

SON OF TARZAN - PRODUCTION PHOTOGRAPH.

1. The Adventures Of Tarzan is said to include another real on-camera lion-killing by Lincoln. Louise Lorraine, the actress who plays love-interest Jane, was fifteen years old when shooting commenced. The serial's chapters were: Jungle Romance; City Of Gold; Sun Death; The Stalking Death; Flames Of Hate; Fangs Of The Lion; The Jungle Trap; The Tornado; The Ivory Tomb; The Simoon; The Hidden Foe; The Dynamite Trail; The Jungle's Fury; Flaming Arrows; and The Last Adventure. It was re-released in 1928 as a 10-chapter edit, with added on-disc sound effects, and again in 1935 as a 10-chapter edit with synchronized sound, and new chapter titles as follows: Tarzan The Fearless; Tarzan's Hideout; Tarzan's Enemies; Tarzan Vanishes; Tarzan Conquers; Tarzan Faces Death; Fighting Tarzan; Cyclone Tarzan; Fangs Vs. Tarzan; and A Message For Tarzan.

2. The fifteen chapters of Son Of Tarzan were: Call Of The Jungle; Out Of The Lion's Jaws; The Girl Of The Jungle; The Sheik's Revenge; The Pirate's Prey; The Killer's Mate; The Quest Of The Killer; Coming Of Tarzan; The Kiss Of The Beast; Tarzan Takes The Trail; Ashes Of Love; Meriem's Ride In The Night; Double Crossed; Blazing Hearts; and An Amazing Denouement.

AZ ÖSEMBER – PRODUCTION PHOTOGRAPH.

AZ ÖSEMBER

("The Primal Man", Cornélius Hintner, 1917-18: Hungary)
Produced by Alfréd Deésy, **Az Ösember** was an allegorical film about evolutionary experiments with apes, in which a hybrid creature named Dominus is created by a deranged scientist using ape-human brain transplants. The narrative is resolved when Dominus, tormented by his intermediary state, is liberated by destroying the human part of his consciousness.

DARWIN. DIE ABSTAMMUNG DES MENSCHEN VOM AFFEN

("Darwin: Man's Descent From The Ape"; Fritz Bernhardt, 1919: Germany)
Hamburg animal hunter/trader-cum-film producer John Hagenbeck"s **Darwin. Die Abstammung Des Menschen Vom Affen** – also released in 1920 as **Darwin – Im Fieber Unter Afrikas Tropensonne** ("Darwin: Fevered Under Africa's Tropical Sun") and as **Das Welträtsel Mensch** ("The Enigma of Man") – was an early example of the miscegenistic ape creature/white girl trope, with poster art showing a woman abducted by a lust-crazed gorilla.

A SCREAM IN THE NIGHT - LOBBY CARD.

A SCREAM IN THE NIGHT
(Burton King & Leander de Cordova, 1919: USA)

At the end-of-decade apex of cumulative and disparate film narratives concerning "jungle girls", "mad scientists", and "killer apes", **A Scream In The Night** combines these pulp elements in the tale of a crazed evolutionary scientist who kidnaps a young girl and raises her as Darwa (after Darwin), a feral denizen of the jungle. After some confusing sub-plots concerning the various parties who come in search of the missing girl, the film reaches its sensational climax – the mad scientist locks Darwa in a cage with a demented, homicidal gorilla, so that when the beast rapes the girl it will prove the link between humans and apes. According to reviews, Darwa escapes by engaging the gorilla in a game of Russian roulette; first she points a pistol – which has only one bullet – at her own head and pulls the trigger. She then hands the pistol to the ape, which mimics her action and fires the only bullet into its own skull. It is not clear why Darwa does not simply shoot the ape herself. **A Scream In the Night** was from a story by Charles A. Logue, and starred acrobat Ruth Budd as Darwa. The actor in the gorilla costume – which appears to be one of the most advanced of its period – was uncredited.

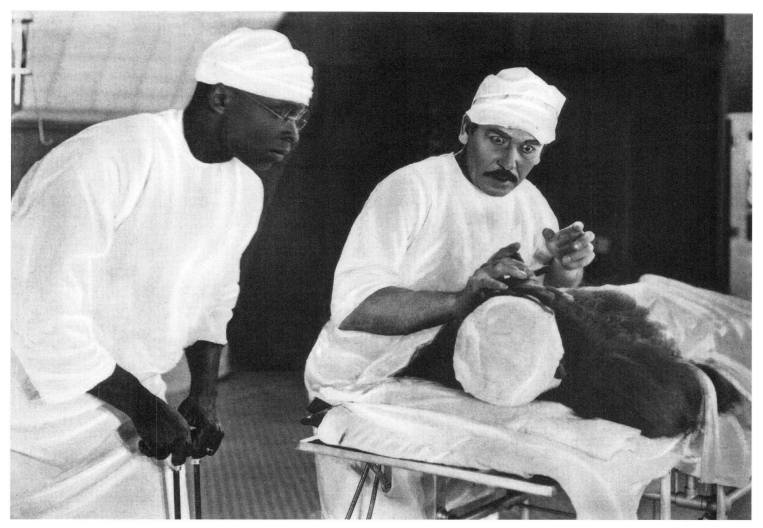

GO AND GET IT – PRODUCTION PHOTOGRAPHS.

GO AND GET IT
(Marshall Neilan & Henry Roberts Symonds, 1920: USA)
A horror-mystery with some unwelcome levity, **Go And Get It** is remembered for the participation of screen heavy Bull Montana, who plays a homicidal ape-human creature – apparently the result of implanting a hanged gangster's brain into a gorilla. Montana's acclaimed make-up, created by Cecil Holland, is exceptionally grotesque; Montana's ape-man stands as one of the early cinema's most hideous apparitions. A series of brutal murders committed by the creature is finally solved by a reporter, uncovering a plot to wreck his newspaper. The premise of human to ape, or ape to human, brain transplantation would become one of horror's – and horror-comedy's – most over-used plot devices. Holland and Montana would famously recreate their ape-man five years later, in Harry O. Hoyt's classic dinosaur fantasy **The Lost World**. Montana also reportedly played an ape-creature (named Monk) in the 15-chapter action serial **Vanishing Millions** (1926), but few details concerning this seemingly lost chapter-play – also featuring Sheldon Lewis and George Kotsonaros – were permanently recorded.[1] In a similar vein to **Go And Get It** was **On Time** (1924), an action-farce starring Richard Talmadge which includes yellow peril villainy and a mad doctor who tries to transplant a gorilla's brain into a man's head. This is one of several episodes in which Talmadge's character is being tested, unwittingly, as a potential movie star. This ending, in which a series of wild adventures are revealed to have been staged, would be repeated in films such as **Seven Footprints To Satan**. **On Time** also features dwarfish actor John George and Tom Wilson, an actor known for blackface roles. Another semi-comedic film with an ape-creature was Warner Brothers' **The Missing Link** (1927), an evolutionary farce starring Syd Chaplin. Played by the hulking Sam Baker, the Link more resembles a furry man-monkey.

VANISHING MILLIONS – PRODUCTION PHOTOGRAPH (*ABOVE*).

THE MISSING LINK – PRODUCTION PHOTOGRAPH (*LEFT*).

THE LOST WORLD – PRODUCTION PHOTOGRAPH (*OPPOSITE PAGE*).

Another notable comedy was James Horne's **Scared Stiff** (1925), a Hal Roach "spooky house" two-reeler written by Stan Laurel and featuring a "monster ape" named Kajanka.[2] A grotesque gorilla, more resembling a man-ape hybrid, could previously be seen in the Monty Banks farce **The Covered Schooner** (1923), while William Fox's **Love And Lions** (1925) boasted the perfect absurdist combination of a fake gorilla, a fake ostrich, a real lion, and an ape-man.

1. George Kotsonaros – a wrestler who played a character called The Bull From Montana in **The Fighting Doctor** (also 1926) – was also known for "ape-man" roles in the films **While London Sleeps** (also 1926) **The Wizard** (1927), and **The Fifty–Fifty Girl** (1928). It remains unconfirmed whether the ape-man in **On Time** was played by Montana, Kotsonaros, or an unknown third party, although existing lobby cards show a close resemblance to Montana's portrayals of such creatures; it should also be noted that Montana reportedly worked on at least one unspecified Talmadge project in 1924.

2. The ape was in fact a normal chimpanzee, seemingly filmed against miniature props to make it seem enormous, and at one point clutching a doll to represent one of the film's female players. This trick-strategy had previously been used by Tod Browning in his freak-horror film **The Unholy Three**, released the previous year, and was employed again in 1926 to a ridiculous degree in **Fig Leaves**, which shows a prehistoric hunter confronted by a towering, 40-foot ape.

WHILE LONDON SLEEPS – MENACED BY THE MONK;
PRODUCTION PHOTOGRAPH.

The SCREAMING SHADOW

(Duke Worne, 1920: USA)

Worne followed his bizarre yellow peril classic **Trail Of The Octopus** with another outlandish 15-chapter serial, this time a horror/SF trip themed around human experiments, in which a mad surgeon attempts to achieve life prolongation by implanting monkey glands, with predictably catastrophic consequences. A scientist, Rand (played by Ben F. Wilson) is sent to investigate, accompanied by a female reporter (played by Neva Gerber); in a remote European country, they discover that the surgeon, Baron Pulska, is conducting human experiments on live patients. Pulska is assisted by Nadia, mysterious high priestess of the temple of eternal youth, whose "virgins" are said to be the first product of the Baron's gland-implantation programme. The plot also includes a millionaire who craves rejuvenation, and heads a secret syndicate known as Eternal Light. As feared, some of Pulska's test subjects do not turn out as hoped; the commingling of ape and human tissue results in hideous hybrid mutations. The Baron's gruesome experiments are finally exposed, and his laboratory destroyed. The serial's chapters were: **A Cry In The Dark; The Virgin Of Death; The Fang Of The Beast; The Black Seven; The Vapor Of Death; The Hidden Menace; Into The Depths; The White Terror; The Sleeping Death; The Prey Of Mong; Liquid Fire; Cold Steel; The Fourth Symbol; Entombed Alive;** and **Unmasked**. A man/ape creature created by gland implantation also figured in **The Great London Mystery** (also 1920), the first British horror-crime serial (the earlier **Ultus** films, although released as a numbered serial in the USA, were actually a series of discrete narratives). Directed by Charles Raymond, **The Great London Mystery** was a 12-chapter "yellow peril" melodrama built around stage illusionist David Devant, who plays a magician dedicated to exposing a Chinese crime cult.[1] The serial includes horror, séances, and a wicked *femme fatale* named Froggy the Vampire.

1. The twelve chapters of **The Great London Mystery** were: **The Sacred Snake Worshippers; The Vengeance Of Ching Fu; The Search For The Will; The Daylight Gold Robbery; The House Of Mystery; Echoes Of The Past; The Rogue Unmasked; The Fraudulent Spiritualistic Seance; The Living Dead; Her Fortune At Stake; Checkmated;** and **East And West**. It was one of the many serials which were also released in France, where it was known as **Le Grand Mystère De Londres**; its twelve episodes were titled: **Le Secret Du Serpent** ("Secret Of The Snake"); **La Vengeance Du Grand Prêtre** ("The High Priest's Revenge"); **Le Testament D'Harry Malvern** ("Harry Malvern's Will"); **Les Voleurs D'Or** ("The Gold-Thieves"); **La Maison Du Mystère** ("House Of Mystery"); **La Confession D'Hélène** ("Helen's Confession"); **L'Héretière Des Millions** ("Heir To Millions"); **Les Faux Spirites** ("The Fake Spirits"); **Les Morts Parlent** ("The Dead Speak"); **La Clef D'Enigme** ("Key To The Riddle"); **Le Sosie Du Grand Prêtre** ("The High Priest's Double"); and **Le Triomphe De Webbs** ("Webbs' Victory").

The EVOLUTION OF MAN

(Nathan Hirsh, 1920: USA)

A film shrouded in mystery, produced by Hirsh, and purporting to prove Darwin's theory of evolution by documenting the manipulation by scheming crooks of an ape-human hybrid known only as The Man-Ape Jack. Few other details of the film seem to have survived, but the film's climax – reportedly featuring a fight at the top of a tower – pre-echoes that of **King Kong**, filmed in 1932. Coincidentally, **The Evolution Of Man** was filmed just after the "discovery" by Swiss geologist François de Loys of a bizarre, tailless, 5-foot simian-anthropoid in Venezuela, circa 1918-1919. Loys' photographed the beast, but it was later dismissed as a hoax. **The Evolution Of Man** also coincided with real-life experiments in mammalian hybridization by the Russian zoologist Ilya Ivanov, whose methods of artificial insemination reportedly resulted in the creation of a freak-beast menagerie which included a cow-antelope and a zebra-donkey. In the 1920s, Ivanov turned his attention to creating the world's first ape-human hybrid. His experiments, sponsored by Josef Stalin, were designed to discredit the claims of organized religion, which Stalin sought to eradicate (some have speculated that Stalin was also interested in the possibility of creating a new breed of super-soldier). When Ivanov's attempts to fertilize female chimpanzees with human sperm proved futile, he turned to the possibility of impregnating women with ape semen. Needless to say, these experiments also resulted in failure (and reputedly the deaths of several "test subjects").

BALI, THE UNKNOWN
(Harold H. Horton, 1921: USA)

An intriguing exotic travelogue, notable as one of the relatively few films – and the first full-length film – made in the Prizma colour process, which was invented in 1913 and lasted until 1923. As such, **Bali, The Unknown** stands as one of the very first colour documentary feature films ever made. Also known by the title **Ape Man Island**, the film ostensibly records an anthropological expedition to find and film the "missing link", or an ape/human hybrid. While Horton almost certainly failed in that respect, he was more than likely compensated by some shots of naked human females. On both counts, **Bali, The Unknown** stands as a definite precursor to the voyeuristic "goona-goona" genre of the 1930s.

MEANDERING IN AFRICA
(Carl Akeley, 1921: USA)

Inventor, explorer, and leading taxidermist, Carl Akeley was also heavily engaged with natural history; in 1915 he had patented the Akeley camera, a mobile device designed specifically for the filming of wildlife in Africa. In 1921, Akeley became the first man to capture in motion pictures one of that continent's most legendary, mysterious and elusive beasts – the giant silverback gorilla.[1] Even in 1921, gorillas were the subject of much lurid speculation, some positing them as the "missing link" between man and beast, others speculating on sexual miscegeny between the rampant gorilla and nymphomaniac African females – the latter myth forming the core of **Ingagi**, a notorious film which would appear several years later. This supposed sexual potency was also evident in Bertram Gayton's *The Gland Stealers* (1922), a satirical novel in which rejuvenation scientists hunt one hundred gorillas, intent on harvesting the beasts' testicles. Akeley's own core mission was to capture and kill a number of specimens from the Belgian Congo, which he intended to stuff and mount in a stunning African diorama at the Museum of Natural History. He ended up shooting dead five mountain gorillas, among them a huge male whom he dubbed "the Giant of Karisimbi", and who would later stand erect at the centre of the diorama.[2] Evidently much affected by his interactions with the gorilla, Akeley would later become a prominent voice for the preservation of the species (hunters, such as the Prince of Sweden, were already taking a heavy toll), and a sanctuary on Mount Mikeno was opened in 1925; Akeley set out for Mikeno in 1926 to make more films, but died from jungle fever during the trip. His corpse was buried there. Akeley was followed into the Kivi region by Ben Burbridge, whose **The Gorilla Hunt** (1926) was an ethno-documentary shot on and around Mount Mikeno in 1924-25; cannibals, pygmies, crocodiles, pythons, natives devouring the raw flesh of a dying elephant, and other now-familiar horrors were also shown in the 5-reel film.[3] Burbridge promoted it with a 5-part article, "The Gorilla Hunt", published in *Forest And Stream*. **Gorilla Hunt** was distributed by Joseph P. Kennedy (whose sons later became prominent in US politics) through FBO. Some sensationalistic advertising for the film promised a "seven-foot gorilla" who "crushes skulls" – presumably referring to the film's highlight, a charge towards the camera by a huge 450-pound male (shown in a promotional photograph in which Burbridge stands next to its corpse, against which are propped two hunting rifles). This specimen was later displayed at the National Museum. Burbridge's **Kidnapping Gorillas** (1933-34) was seemingly a sound update, possibly with additional footage, by distributors Kinematrade. Burbridge, who also wrote a book entitled *Gorilla: Tracking And Capturing The Ape-Man Of Africa* (1928, a title which seems to endorse the "missing link" theory), was known to train his primate captives by beating and whipping them. His most famous, a female named Congo, was eventually sold to Ringling's Circus.

1. Akeley's other significant contribution to film history in 1921 was the facilitation of Martin and Osa Johnson's first African expedition, setting in motion a 16-year cycle of film-making which would produce some of the most famous jungle documentaries of all time.

2. Akeley was not averse to animal slaughter; in 1910, he had reportedly staged and restaged a lion-spearing ritual for the movie cameras, resulting in the impalement death of almost twenty big cats. Recounting this venture in his 1926 pamphlet *Lion Spearing*, published by the Chicago Field Museum of Natural History, Akeley describes a leopard corpse punctured by sixty spear-holes.

THE GORILLA HUNT – FILM POSTER, AFTER FREMIET'S
GORILLE ENLEVANT UNE FEMME.

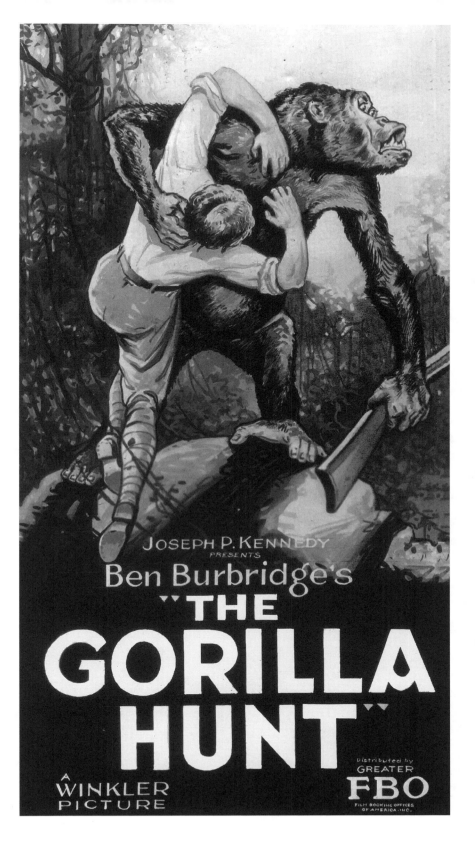

3. Fake scenes included Burbridge grappling with a gorilla, which was in fact his son in an ape costume. Another film entitled **The Gorilla Hunt** was seemingly also in circulation, or at least in production, which featured stop-motion model animation by J.L. Roop. Some have suggested that's Roop's work was in fact for an insert into Burbridge's film, but this is not confirmed. Roop's previous films had included **The Jungle Of Prehistoric Animals** (1924), a little-known dinosaur animation. Ub Iwerks' **The Gorilla Hunt** (1939) was a **Color Rhapsody** cartoon for Columbia, in which a game-hunter presents a film within a film of his African exploits, with scenes of bone-haired savages and a huge, slavering silverback.

A BLIND BARGAIN – PRODUCTION PHOTOGRAPHS.

A BLIND BARGAIN
(Wallace Worsley, 1922: USA)

Produced by Samuel Goldwyn, starring Lon Chaney, and based on the novel *The Octave Of Claudius* by Barry Pain, **A Blind Bargain** was the most *outré* US horror film of the year, a 60-minute nightmare of surgical terror and transmutation. Chaney plays a dual role, portraying both the mad surgeon Dr. Lamb, and his hunch-backed, simian assistant. Lamb's deranged experiments aim to create an ape-human hybrid (a plot device based on the real-life theories of Serge Voronoff, whose medical procedures involved transplanting monkey glands into humans, in an attempt to stimulate rejuvenation). When his latest intended victim is shown an array of hideous mutant creatures kept in cages – previous experiments, of which the deformed assistant is one – he attempts to flee, but is overpowered by the doctor. The hunchback releases a huge ape-creature which crushes the life from its creator. Another film inspired by Serge Voronoff was **Black Oxen** (1923), based on a novel of the same name, but it lacked the horrific power of **A Blind Bargain**. In 1922, it would have been impossible to replicate on screen the full horrors of Voronoff's actual experiments, which also included transplanting the testicles of executed criminals into ageing patients, inserting monkey ovaries into women, and performing skin grafts of monkey testicle tissue. Voronoff, a French physician of Russian origin, first began human medical experimentation during WWI, using bone grafts to treat the wounded. He later founded the Voronoff Foundation, where his experimental program of transplanting the glands and testicles of primates into humans was carried out. A number of Voronoff's experiments were documented on film; he recorded surgical demonstrations of testicular transplants and screened them at medical conventions in Paris, Bruxelles, and Sevilla in the period from 1924-25. His practices also extended to "curing" homosexuals by grafting monkey testicle tissue inside their scrotums, and skin rejuvenation using foetal membrane. It is said that at the height of demand for his services, Voronoff had his own monkey farm in Italy, run by circus trainers, for the harvesting of simian genitalia. A Russian Krasnaya Zvezda ("Red Star") science-film from 1925, **Kogo Nuzhno Omolazhivat?** ("Who Needs Rejuvenation?"), also dealt with testicular transplantation; its promotional poster, illustrated by the Sternberg brothers, shows an old man undergoing genital surgery (with text covering the crucial incision site). The film was directed by Leonid Voskresenskiy, a former student of Ivan Pavlov, who became a disciple of Voronoff and an advocate of sex gland transplantation. Voskresenskiy reportedly appeared at screenings of his film and delivered lectures on rejuvenation, to much acclaim. He also filmed behavioural and neurological experiments with apes – particularly hamadryas baboons – at Sukhumi, a breeding station in Georgia established in 1923. One of the other notable films made there was A.V. Vinnitskiy's **Obezyany I Chelovek** ("Monkeys And Men", 1930), espousing a Marxist theory of evolution. During WWII, Sukhumi also proved an invaluable source of primate test-subjects for medical vaccines which saved the lives of countless Soviet soldiers.

The LAST MOMENT
(J. Parker Read Jr., 1923: USA)
A bizarre horror-tinged film set on a ship whose brutal captain keeps control of his shanghai'ed crew with the threat of unleashing the ape-creature caged below (played by Jerry Peterson). When this monster escapes during a storm and slaughters its captors, the surviving couple must somehow head to shore before becoming its final prey...

LORRAINE OF THE LIONS
(Edward Sedgwick, 1925: USA)
A jungle-girl narrative starring Patsy Ruth Miller and notable for the appearance of Fred Humes as a gorilla. Humes, one of Hollywood's first gorilla men, later teamed up with another Lorraine – serial action star Louise Lorraine – to play Bimbo, a trained gorilla, in MGM's light-hearted **Circus Rookies** (1928).

LORRAINE OF THE LIONS – PRODUCTION PHOTOGRAPH (*OPPOSITE TOP*).
CIRCUS ROOKIES – PRODUCTION PHOTOGRAPH (*OPPOSITE BOTTOM*).

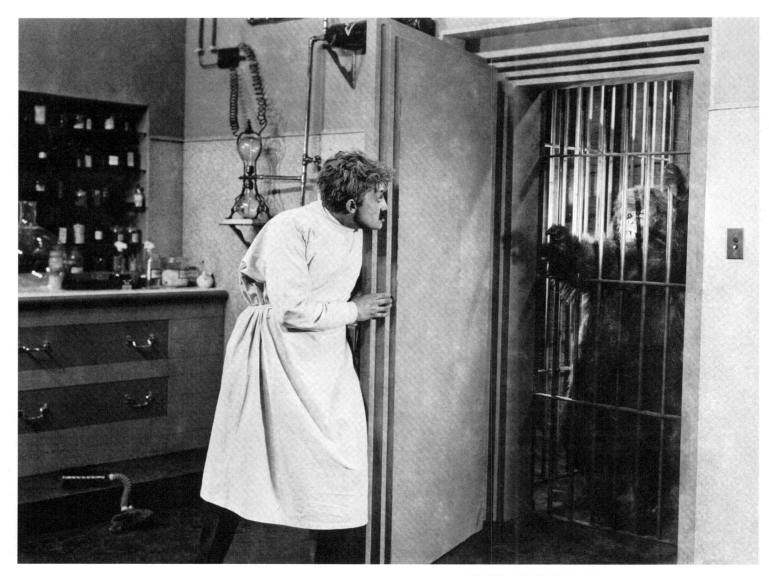

RED LIGHTS

(Clarence C. Badger, 1923: USA)

A weird mystery that climaxes on a speeding train, with a hooded maniac using red hypno-lights to transmit flashing death threats to the heroine even as a "crime deflecting" sleuth is hot on his trail. A crazed gorilla is also on board the locomotive, which becomes a mobile version of the "murder mansion" complete with secret compartments and hidden traps. **Red Lights** was based on the 1922 mystery play *The Rear Car* by Edward E. Rose. Equally bizarre was a 1933 sound remake, MGM's **Murder In The Private Car**, which took the original concept to extremes.

KAIBUTSU

("Monster"; Bansho Kanamori, 1925: Japan)

From Toa Tojin, **Kaibutsu** – a 2-part mystery film in the **Saheiji Torimonocho** ("Detective Saheiji Casebook") series – was one of the first Japanese films to feature a monster-ape, in this case a circus freak (played by Shinpei Takagi) who appears to be responsible for a glut of savage murders in old Edo. Another monster-ape film was the same film company's **Gorira** ("Gorilla", 1926), the tale of a Japanese scholar who learns *yojutsu* ("black magic") from an ancient Dutch grimoire and transforms himself into a human-ape hybrid, embarking on a rampage of murderous revenge against those who have wronged him. Kawai Eiga's **Gorira** (1933) was a similar story of human into ape metamorphosis and slaughter. Nikkatsu's **Yokai No Sumu Ie** ("House Where Monsters Dwell", 1925) also featured a gorilla-man, as well as various other shadowy figures including a prostitute, a gangster, and his hunchbacked henchman. A man-beast was also the title creature of Shinpei Pro's **Kaiketsu Oni** ("Super-Devil", 1927), while Takarazuka Eiga's **Kaiketsu Arahoshi** ("Super-Priest", 1933) was a 2-part film in which a violent *samurai* family quarrel is joined by not only the wild priest of the title, but also by a giant ape-creature.

KAIKETSU ARAHOSHI – PRODUCTION PHOTOGRAPH (*ABOVE*).
KAIBUTSU – PRODUCTION PHOTOGRAPH (*OVERLEAF VERSO*).
GORIRA (1926) – PRODUCTION PHOTOGRAPH (*OVERLEAF RECTO*).

TAILORING – PRODUCTION PHOTOGRAPH.

TAILORING

(James D. Davis, 1925: USA)

In 1925, producer Joe Rock – perhaps inspired by the midget comedies of the previous decade – assembled his own freak-farce team of obese slapstick stars comprising Hilliard "Fat" Karr, Frank "Fatty" Alexander and "Kewpie" Ross, each weighing more than 300 pounds. This trio – billed as Three Fat Men or Ton of Fun – made a series of around thirty-six short films for FBO over the following three years, starting with **Tailoring** and including **Galloping Ghosts** (1926), a spook-episode. Some say that Rock even made the trio wear extra padding, in order to accentuate their obesity into the realms of delirium. **Tailoring** is most notable for featuring a grotesque ape costume, an indicator that the cinema of animal impersonations would soon become dominated by one great beast – the gorilla.

UNKNOWN TREASURES – PRODUCTION PHOTOGRAPH.

UNKNOWN TREASURES
(Archie Mayo, 1926: USA)

Adapted from a story entitled "The House Behind The Hedge" by Mary Spain Vigus – a sparsely-published romance writer during the 1920s – **Unknown Treasures** is a generic "dark house" thriller involving murder, financial misdemeanours, and an ancient home haunted by a madman and his homicidal pet, a bizarre mutant gorilla-creature. The hero's valet, a dice-addicted "coon", is played by a white actor in blackface; the actor who plays the grotesque killer ape is not credited. **Unknown Treasures** finds its place among the decade's many such films, perhaps somewhat elevated due to the exceptionally frightful appearance of its hominid haunter, a figure torn from the pages of Poe, and one which predates the less outlandish beast seen in 1927's **The Gorilla**.

DELUGE:
THE GOLDEN AGE OF
GORILLA MEN 1927–1949

The GORILLA
(Afred Santell, 1927: USA)

Ralph Spence's mystery play *The Gorilla* debuted on Broadway in 1925; the story is set in an archetypal old dark house of trap-doors, sliding panels and weird lights, where a savage murder (one of several by the Gorilla, who boasts of killing men and kidnapping – in other words raping – women) is blamed on a homicidal ape. The ape (played by John Phillip Kolb) turns out to be a sailor in costume, while the true killer is revealed as another of those gathered in the midnight proceedings. The film version was produced by First National, and proved an influential marker in the "murder mansion" genre – both for the inclusion of shambling jungle-beasts and, less fortunately, in adding comic relief. Charles Gemora,[1] who designed the film's gorilla suit, wore one himself in Bryan Foy's 1930 remake (again for First National); the film was remade yet again in 1939 by Fox, with Bela Lugosi as a creepy butler and Art Miles, another leading gorilla impersonator, as the marauding ape. Of the three versions, Santell's least dilutes the play's underlying horror-mystery, while the remakes are progessively blended with comedic elements. **Sh! The Octopus** (1937), a Warner Brothers mystery set in a lighthouse – and first announced for production by First National in 1928 – is also said to derive largely from Spence's original, but replaces the ape with a giant sea-monster. Cartoon producers were also quick to tap into the Hollywood vogue for mystery-horror films featuring rampaging killer-

THE GORILLA (1930) – PRODUCTION PHOTOGRAPHS (*ABOVE & OVERLEAF VERSO*).

THE GORILLA (1939) – PRODUCTION PHOTOGRAPHS (*OVERLEAF RECTO*).

gorillas, notably Walt Disney with his 1930 short **The Gorilla Mystery** in which Mickey Mouse's girlfriend Minnie is abducted and threatened with implied rape-murder by a slavering escaped silverback. Charles Gemora's first films wearing his own gorilla suit included several threatening male specimens in horror, mystery or jungle thrillers such as **The Leopard Lady** (1927), **Tarzan The Mighty** (1928 – a particularly malevolent-featured costume), the weird adventure **Stark Mad** (1929), and Benjamin Christensen's **Seven Footprints To Satan** (1929). He also appeared in large number of comedy shorts, starting with the Lloyd Hamilton "haunted house" farce **Goose Flesh** (1927 – probably his gorilla-suit debut). He also appeared in a number of short films for Hal Roach, including **Do Gentlemen Snore?** (1928) and two **Our Gang** romps, **The Holy Terror** (1929) and **Bear Shooters** (1930). Although many of Gemora's appearances were uncredited, he is also thought to be behind the gorilla mask in several other short farces of this period such as Orville Dull's **His Favourite Wife** (Fox, 1928), the Christie production **Why Gorillas Leave Home** (1929), and Educational's **His Baby Daze** (1929, with Lloyd Hamilton again, and also starring midget actor "Little" Billy Rhodes). A less impressive gorilla suit could be seen in several Mack Sennett comedies of this period, most notably **Taxi Spooks** (1929), set in a haunted house.[2]

1. Of Filipino origin, Gemora started in Hollywood as a set sculptor; his work can be seen in **The Phantom Of The Opera** (1925) and numerous other productions.

2. One of a 6-film series directed by Del Lord and starring Jack Cooper as a wayward cab driver; the others in the series were **A Taxi Scandal** (1928), **Taxi For Two** (1928), **Taxi Beauties** (1928), **Taxi Dolls** (1929, with a robot), and **Caught In A Taxi** (1929).

CHARLES GEMORA SCULPTING A BUST OF ACTOR RICARDO CORTEZ FOR THE GANGSTER FILM **BAD COMPANY** – PRODUCTION PHOTOGRAPH, 1931 (*BELOW*).

HIS BABY DAZE – PRODUCTION PHOTOGRAPH (*OPPOSITE PAGE*).

DO GENTLEMEN SNORE? – PRODUCTION PHOTOGRAPH (*OVERLEAF VERSO TOP*); **THE HOLY TERROR** – PRODUCTION PHOTOGRAPH (*OVERLEAF VERSO BOTTOM*).

BEAR SHOOTERS – PRODUCTION PHOTOGRAPH (*OVERLEAF RECTO*).

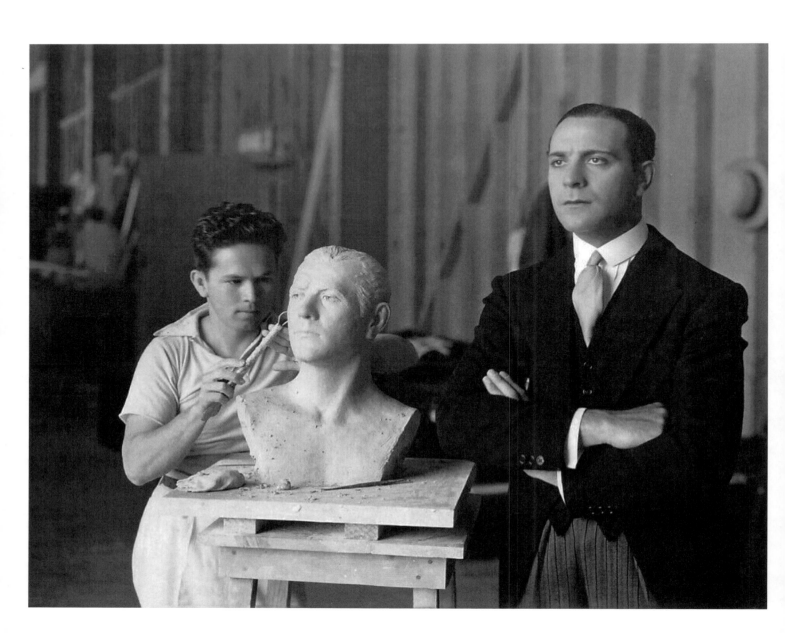

ISLE OF SUNKEN GOLD
(Harry S. Webb, 1927: USA)

As the 1920s progressed, many serial-makers gradually pulled away from the reckless violence, murder and mayhem of the classic period, moving from the visceral towards the more circumspect. This sorry slackening would be somewhat redressed by the formation in 1927 of Nat Levine's Mascot Pictures, a poverty row studio[1] whose first wave of plot-twisted, pulp-oriented serials began in earnest with **Isle Of Sunken Gold**, a 10-chapter pirate-treasure escapade made interesting by the inclusion of the "Devil-Ape of Bomo". This gorilla-creature, described as a "mysterious missing link", is a huge fanged monster worshipped by island savages, which dwells in a volcanic cave and serves Princess Kala (played by Anita Stewart). The serial's chapters were: **Isle Of Sunken Gold; Trapped In Mid-Air; Engulfed By The Sea; The Volcano's Pit; The Hulk Of Death; The Prey Of Sharks; Fire Of Revenge; The Battle Of Canoes; Trapped By The Ape;** and **The Devil Ape's Secret**. The influence of serials such as **Isle Of Sunken Gold** can be seen in such referential comedies of the time as Mermaid's **Leaping Luck** (1928), an exceptionally grotesque slapstick 2-reeler set on an island with a sinister underground sect and marauding, man-eating crocodiles.

1. The term "poverty row" was applied to various small independent film studios in Hollywood in the 1920s and 1930s; one of the very first was Rayart Pictures, a production and distribution company founded in 1924, which ran until 1930 before being assimilated. Rayart produced and/or distributed several low-budget serials, of which the weirdest was the 10-chapter **Phantom Police** (1926), notable for featuring a pair of performing chimps named Max and Moritz. The serial's 2-reel chapters are not confirmed by title in copyright records, but included **Midnight Patrol** and **Daring Doom**. It was written and directed by Robert Dillon. Apart from Mascot, some of the other active poverty row studios were Majestic, Monogram, Chesterfield, Reliable, Progressive, Superior, Syndicate, Liberty, Chadwick, Tiffany, and Victory. Most of them had faded away by the 1950s.

THE PHANTOM POLICE – CHIMPS MAX AND MORITZ AS POLICE OFFICERS; PRODUCTION PHOTOGRAPH.
THE CHIMPS WERE TRAINED BY REUBEN CASTANG, FORMERLY WITH HAGENBECK'S CIRCUS; CASTANG'S ORIGINAL MAX AND MORITZ HAD DIED DURING WORLD WAR I AFTER BEING SEPARATED FROM CASTANG WHEN HE WAS IMPRISONED IN RUHLEBEN, GERMANY'S NOTORIOUS, RAT-INFESTED CIVILIAN DETENTION CAMP.

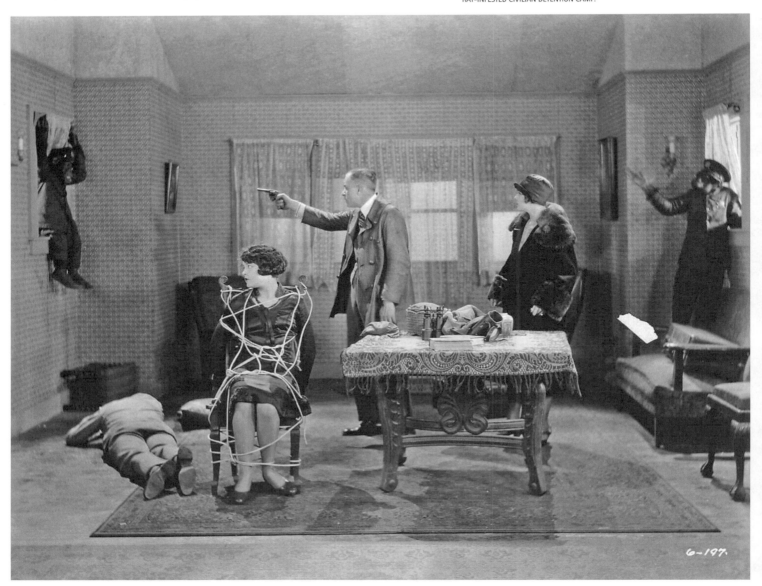

6-197.

THE LEOPARD LADY – PRODUCTION PHOTOGRAPHS (*ABOVE & BELOW RIGHT*); DIRECTOR RUPERT JULIAN WITH CHARLES GEMORA IN GORILLA COSTUME; PUBLICITY PHOTOGRAPH (*BELOW*).

The LEOPARD LADY
(Rupert Julian, 1927: USA)
Released at the beginning of 1928, this DeMille Pictures production stands alongside other weird circus/sideshow films of the period, primarily due to its Poe-influenced plot of a great ape (gorilla) trained to kill by its criminal master (in this case, a Cossack animal trainer). Jacqueline Logan is the "leopard lady" assigned to investigate the beast's spate of thefts and killings. In an ending similar to that of **A Scream In the Night** (1919), the gorilla is finally induced to bring about its own demise. Charles Gemora, perhaps the most renowned of all gorilla impersonators, here makes his dramatic (as opposed to comedic) debut in costume as the murderous ape. Based on a 1925 play by Edward Childs Carpenter.

RAMPER, DER TIERMENSCH – PRODUCTION PHOTOGRAPH.

RAMPER, DER TIERMENSCH
("Ramper, The Beast-Man"; Max Reichmann, 1927: Germany)
Paul Wegener's weirdest film of the late silent era, in which he plays Captain Ramper, an aviator stranded in the Arctic. He survives alone for fifteen years, but his body adapts to the extreme cold by growing a coarse layer of fur-like hair; he also forgets how to speak. When Ramper is finally discovered by a passing whaling ship, the crew believe him to be some kind of "missing link" between animal and human. In a plot device which anticipates the tragic denouement of **King Kong** a few years later, Ramper is taken back to civilisation and immediately sold as a sideshow exhibit. When his true status as a human is finally confirmed, he receives financial compensation but gives it away, preferring to return, Frankenstein-like, to his solitary existence in the ice wastes. Despite its unlikely premise, **Ramper, Der Tiermensch** exerts an exotic fascination, augmented by the rare participation of **Nosferatu** actor Max Schreck in hallucination scenes, in which he essays symbolic personifications of various extremes (cold, hunger, and other neural persecutions). As for Wegener, his make-up recalls a hybrid of the various hypertrichotics and hirsute albinos who starred in circus and freakshows of the day, such as Jo-Jo the Dog-Boy or Tom-Jack the Ice King (an albino escapologist) – perhaps deliberately so, given Ramper's eventual incarceration as an exhibit.

THE WIZARD – LOBBY CARD.

The WIZARD
(Richard Rossen, 1927: USA)

Produced by Fox under the working title of **Balaoo**, Rossen's surgical horror film was based on the pulp horror-novel of that title by Gaston Leroux, in which a deranged scientist creates an intelligent ape-human hybrid (a story first filmed in 1913 by Victorin-Hippolyte Jasset). In **The Wizard**, the scientist creates a monstrous ape-man for the explicit purpose of exacting vengeance upon the judge and prosecutor who sent his son to the electric chair; once all the protagonists are gathered at the judge's house by night, the grim drama unfolds, with mysterious disappearances and a climactic confrontation with the murderous creature. The last known print of **The Wizard** was said to be one of hundreds of films destroyed by a calamitous Fox vault fire which ignited in 1937; surviving photographs indicate an atmosphere of mystery and weird horror enhanced by exaggerated shadows and angles, and compounded by the exceptionally hideous appearance of the ape-monster (played by George Kotsonaros), which resembles a gorilla with a human face-graft. Leroux's story would be filmed again in 1942, again by Fox, under the new title **Dr. Renault's Secret.**

The MONKEY TALKS
(Raoul Walsh, 1927: USA)

Circus and sideshow films formed a distinct and often bizarre sub-genre in the first decades of cinema; a prime example from 1927 was **The Monkey Talks**, involving a love triangle between a tightrope walker (luscious starlet Olive Borden), a man who pretends to be a talking chimpanzee in his act, and the man who plays his trainer. When a "real" ape also becomes involved (also a man in a monkey suit), the stage is set for a showdown of violent human-primate erotomania.

The APE
(B.C. Rule, 1928: USA)

The Ape remains one of the most elusive of all silent mystery movies. The film was said to be based on "actual police records", but very little else about this shadowy work is confirmed save that it was a low-budget, low-quality effort, dealing with crimes by an apparently non-human killer.

BO-RU, THE APE BOY
(Dwain Esper, 1929-34: USA)

Dwain Esper, one of cinema's most enterprising and creative roadshow hustlers, created this jungle feature by cutting down and splicing footage from other movies then adding a new narrative, as was his standard practice. The main source for **Bo-Ru, The Ape Boy** was **Stampede**, an ethnographic documentary filmed by Chaplin Court-Treatt, Stella Court-Treatt and Errol Hinds in 1929. Shot in the Sudan, **Stampede** is actually a fictionalized account of an adopted native boy, Boru, who rises to power. The narrative is intercut with "exotic" sequences directly comparing natives to wild animals, and footage of both male and female specimens running naked. It was doubtless this latter facet which appealed to Esper, who in 1934 cut the film down to its 35-minute essentials, added a prurient warning on the dangers of animal/human miscegeny, and presented it as the tale of a feral child raised by apes.

KONG GU YUAN SHENG
("Screaming Ape In The Valley Of Death"; Ma-Xu Weibang, 1930: China)

Ground-breaking writer/director Ma-Xu, whose Hun Shi Mo Wang ("The Devil Incarnate", 1929) was hailed as the first Chinese horror film, went on to create **Kong Gu Yuan Sheng** as a tribute to the "mad ape" movies of Hollywood, with a plot involving kidnapped females, organ transplants, rejuvenation experiments and, of course, a man dressed as a gorilla.

TARZAN THE MIGHTY

(Jack Nelson & Ray Taylor , 1928: USA)

The first of two 15-chapter Tarzan serials from Universal,[1] both starring Frank Merrill (replacing Joe Bonomo, who fractured a leg prior to shooting) as Tarzan and Natalie Kingston as Jane – the second serial was **Tarzan The Tiger** (1929),[2] notable for nude swimming scenes by Kingston aa well as topless nudity in slave-market scenes. Both serials featured sequences with actors in gorilla suits, with an extremely vicious-looking specimen named Taug in **Tarzan The Mighty** being played by Charles Gemora. Gemora returned in **Tarzan The Tiger** to play another dangerous ape, named Taglat. Physically bested by Tarzan, Taglat takes revenge by ambushing and abducting Jane, presumably in order to subject her to trans-species rape. **Tarzan The Mighty** is said to have been based upon the short story collection *Jungle Tales Of Tarzan*, published in 1919, and pits Tarzan against a villain named Black John. The serial's fifteen chapters of were: **The Terror Of Tarzan; The Love Cry; The Call Of The Jungle; The Lion's Leap; Flames Of Hate; The Fiery Pit; The Leopard's Lair; The Jungle Traitor; Lost In The Jungle; Jaws Of Death; A Thief In The Night; The Enemy Of Tarzan; Perilous Paths; Facing Death;** and **The Reckoning.** Based on Edgar Rice Burroughs' 1916 novel *Tarzan And The Jewels Of Opar*, **Tarzan The Tiger**

featured a lost civilization with a malevolent High Priestess, played by an exotic Eurasian dancer named Kithnou. It was released both as silent and with partial sound, the latter with jungle sound effects and the very first "jungle scream" of Tarzan. A third serial starring Frank Merrill – **Tarzan The Terrible**, based on Burroughs' 1921 novel of a hidden valley with dinosaurs and demi-human tribes – was projected but cancelled, possibly due to Universal's concerns over the transition to sound which would be required of the actor. Merrill had previously starred in **Perils Of The Jungle** (1927, directed by Harry L. Fraser),[3] a 10-chapter serial from Louis Weiss which included a feral ape-man creature and cannibal tiger-men amongst its low-budget attractions. Weiss' productions were known as bottom-of-the-barrel circuit fodder, and years later Weiss and Fraser even cut up their own negative of **Perils Of the Jungle** to use as stock footage in a new, hallucinatory montage entitled **White Gorilla**. Former Tarzan Elmo Lincoln also returned to the cinematic jungle scene in 1927, starring in a cash-in serial, Webster Cullison's 10-chapter **The King Of The Jungle**;[4] it is reported that actor Gordon Standing was attacked and killed by a lion during filming, resulting in Lincoln's decision to quit the movie business (he returned a decade later).

1. The Universal serials were immediately preceded by **Tarzan And The Golden Lion** (FBO, 1927), a feature based on Burroughs' 1923 novel of that name and starring James Pierce as Tarzan. The film, which was not commercially successful, notably featured Boris Karloff as Owaza, a jungle savage with a human skull emblazoned upon his head-dress, as well as a Chinese giant named Lin-Yu-Ching who was claimed to be eight feet tall.

2. The fifteen chapters of **Tarzan The Tiger** were: **Call Of The Jungle**; **The Road To Opar**; **The Altar Of The Flaming God**; **The Vengeance Of La**; **Condemned To Death**; **Tantor The Terror**; **The Deadly Peril**; **Loop Of Death**; **Flight Of Werper**; **Prisoner Of The Apes**; **The Jaws Of Death**; **The Jewels Of Opar**; **A Human Sacrifice**; **Tarzan's Rage**; and **Tarzan's Triumph**. It was directed by Henry MacRae.

3. The ten chapters of **Perils of The Jungle** were: **Jungle Trails**; **The Jungle King**; **The Elephant's Revenge**; **At The Lion's Mercy**; **The Sting Of Death**; **The Trail Of Blood**; **The Feast Of Vengeance**; **The Leopards' Attack**; **The Tiger Men** (also known as **The Gorilla's Bride**); and **One-Eyed Monsters** (also known as **The Tiger's Den**).

4. The ten chapters of **The King Of The Jungle** were: **A Great Tragedy**; **The Elephant Avenger**; **Battling For Her Life**; **Into The Lion's Jaws**; **The Striped Terror**; **Gripped By The Death Vice**; **The Slinking Demons**; **The Giant Ape Strikes**; **No Escape**; and **The Death Trap**. Movie heavy George Kotsonaros reprised his usual role as a violent brute-man.

WHERE EAST IS EAST
(Tod Browning, 1929: USA)

Browning and Lon Chaney present their final lurid film collaboration, set in Indo-China. Chaney plays Tiger Haynes, a heavily scarred animal-trapper, and Mexican starlet Lupe Velez features as his daughter; when the girl's estranged mother tries to seduce her fiancée, Tiger lets loose his trained, homicidal gorilla, leading to a climax of carnage. Some sources credit Richard Neill, a bit-part player, as the actor in the gorilla-suit, which resembles those designed by Charles Gemora.

THE APE MAN – SCENE FROM CHAPTER 7 OF THE FIRE
DETECTIVE; PRODUCTION PHOTOGRAPH.

The FIRE DETECTIVE
(Spencer Gordon Bennet & Thomas Storey, 1929: USA)
The criminals in this 10-chapter Pathé mystery-crime serial are a gang of deadly
arsonists, who engage the help of scientists to produce advanced devices and methods
of fire-starting. The most bizarre of these creations is a genetically-engineered human-
ape hybrid, who is able to scale tall buildings and spread fire across the rooftops.
From a story by Frank Leon Smith, the serial's chapters were: **The Arson Trail; The
Pit Of Darkness; The Hidden Hand; The Convict Strikes; On Flaming Waters; The
Man Of Mystery; The Ape Man; Back From Death; Menace Of The Past;** and **The
Flame Of Love.** This would prove to be one of Pathé's very last serials; whilst the
other film companies scrambled to make the transition to sound, Pathé simply
decided not to bother. By the beginning of 1931, the company was gone – merged
with a recently-formed sound production and distribution corporation, RKO
Pictures.

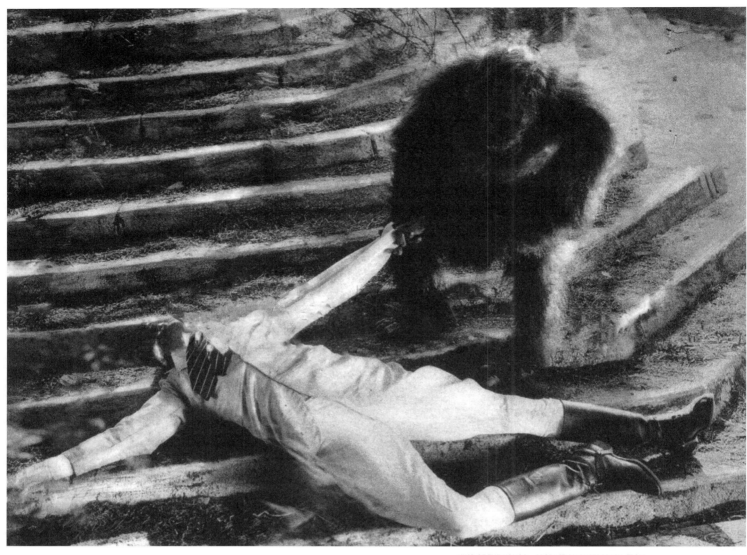

KING OF THE KONGO – PRODUCTION PHOTOGRAPH, FROM PRINTED LOBBY CARD.

KING OF THE KONGO
(Richard Thorpe, 1929: USA)

The last noteworthy 1920s serials with a jungle setting included Mascot's 10-chapter **King Of The Kongo**, said to be the first serial shot with partial sound, and featuring Boris Karloff as a character named Scarface Macklin, plus one of the earliest ape impersonations essayed by stuntman/actor Joe Bonomo, who would often double for Charles Gemora.[1] Produced by Mascot, **King Of The Kongo** was shot on an impressive ruined temple set, and augmented by additional stock footage. The temple is guarded by a hulking gorilla, and a kind of giant mutant lizard is also featured (possibly meant to be a dinosaur). The serial's chapters were: **Into The Unknown; Terrors Of The Jungle; Temple Of Beasts; Gorilla Warfare; Danger In The Dark; Man Of Mystery; The Fatal Moment; Sentenced To Death; Desperate Choices**; and **Jungle Justice**. Boris Karloff's next serial appearance was as a murderous Arab sheikh in Mascot's 12-chapter **King Of The Wild** (1931),[2] set in North Africa; as well as portraying Arabs as villainous scum and native blacks as gibbering primitives, this mystery-crime thriller featured a weird, ape-like creature named Bimi (played by English bit-part actor Arthur McLaglen). It was among the very first wave of all-sound serials – as was Universal's **Danger Island** (1931),[3] another jungle mystery set in Africa. Filmed in twelve chapters, **Danger Island** revolves around the control of a radium mine, and includes a monster orang-utan as well as voodoo-style black magic rituals.

1. As the demand for monster-gorillas in all types of movies steadily increased, other regular gorilla-suit wearers would include Fred Humes, Jack Leonard, Clarence Morehouse, Ray Corrigan, Emil van Horn, Art Miles, and Steve Calvert.

2. The twelve chapters of **King Of The Wild** were: **Man Eaters**; **Tiger Of Destiny**; **The Avenging Horde**; **Secret Of The Volcano**; **Pit Of Peril**; **Creeping Doom**; **Sealed Lips**; **Jaws Of The Jungle**; **Door Of Dread**; **Leopard's Lair**; **The Fire Of The Gods**; and **Jungle Justice**. Richard Thorpe directed.

3. The twelve chapters of **Danger Island** were: **The Coast Of Peril**; **Death Rides The Storm**; **Demons Of The Pool**; **Devil Worshippers**; **Mutiny**; **The Cat Creeps**; **The Drums Of Doom**; **Human Sacrifice**; **The Devil Bird**; **Captured For Sacrifice**; **The Lion's Lair**; and **Fire God's Vengeance**. Ray Taylor directed.

SEVEN FOOTPRINTS TO SATAN

(Benjamin Christensen, 1929: USA)

The "Satan" in **Seven Footprints To Satan** is not the Devil, but a sinister cult leader who revels in infernal regalia. Created by pulp novelist A.E. Merritt, Satan was originally an evil super-villain in the same mould as Sax Rohmer's Fu Manchu – unfortunately, this film version of Merritt's eponymous novel considerably alters the story, and ends in anti-climax. Nevertheless, Christensen does his best with this mandate, creating some magnificent sets – such as Satan's throne room with its huge bat-winged dragons – and manages to include some truly grotesque figures, including a scurrying dwarf (Angelo Rossitto), a monkey-faced savant, a facially deformed hag, and a feral, crippled creature known as The Spider (Sheldon Lewis). Charles Gemora also appears, in his customary role as a vicious gorilla, the Beast of Satan. Satan's mansion is a house of sliding panels and secret corridors, of kidnapped and tortured girls, of sinister freaks, of orgiastic devil-worshippers; scenes include a girl being chained and whipped, her legs held fast by the gorilla. The film is finally let down by its tame ending, imposed by the producers, which reveals the whole thing to have been a "prank", a device often used to condescendingly reassure audiences in much the same way as elements of "comic relief" were often jarringly inserted to ruin otherwise potent horror movies.

STARK MAD
(Lloyd Bacon, 1929: USA)

One of many films issued as both silent and with limited sound, **Stark Mad** is one of the first features to showcase ape impersonator Charles Gemora as a sinister, monstrous gorilla (as opposed to the more comic variety which he played in a number of shorts). The film is set in the Mayan jungles of Central America, where a man launches the search for his missing son. Sheltering in an ancient temple, the man and his team discover a secret chamber where a massive gorilla is chained to the floor. This creature is the slave of a crazed hermit, who murdered the man's son. The temple ruins soon become a death maze, with members of the expedition either shot by arrows or abducted by the vicious beast. Lighter moments were doubtless provided by the presence of comic actress Louise Fazenda. With its exotic location and homicidal gorilla, **Stark Mad** is one of several films which prefigured the ultimate monster ape movie, **King Kong**. Another bizarre ape movie of 1929 was the little-known **The Devil Bear**, a Canadian production in which a ship-wrecked gorilla saves his master from various perils, including native Indians who believe the gorilla is some kind of monstrous bear; it is unconfirmed which actor lurked within the animal costume, although the suit is almost certainly one of Gemora's once again.

TRADER HOUND – FAKE GORILLA AND LION FIGHT;
PRODUCTION PHOTOGRAPH.

TRADER HOUND

(Jules White, 1931: USA)

Following the success of jungle melodrama **Trader Horn**, MGM released its own 2-reel parody **Trader Hound**, destined to be the last in their notorious **Dogville Comedies**, a series which between 1929 and 1931 offered around nine films all enacted by trained dogs and overdubbed with human voices.[1] Bizarre enough to begin with, **Trader Hound** also features animated insects and human actors dressed up in jungle animal costumes, including a lion, gorilla and giraffe. The film was banned outright by the British censors, who clearly felt faint at the very suggestion of cannibal canines, no matter how absurd the context. This helped bring a close to the **Dogville Comedies**, which had also faced mounting accusations of animal cruelty with some critics asserting that scenes where the dogs walked on their hind legs or performed other actions like humans were achieved by trussing their limbs with chicken wire and controlling them like puppets.

1. Hal Roach was among the first to realize this concept, using a variety of monkeys and other creatures as actors in his **Dippy-Doo-Dads** series (1922-24). **Dogville Comedies** was rivalled by a similar series from Tiffany, **Tiffany's Talking Chimps**, which ran for some ten episodes between 1930 and 1931.

INGAGI – THE GORILLA'S RAPE-ATTACK; PRODUCTION
PHOTOGRAPH.

INGAGI
(William Campbell, 1930: USA)
Notorious exploitational hoax-film, a faked documentary of giant gorillas, topless human sacrifice and nude native women. Concocted by William Campbell, a journeyman director of comedy shorts, and ape-mad writer Adam Shirk, **Ingagi** propelled the notion of exotic cinema into a new zone of transgression where everything was counterfeit and nothing was sacred; jungle scenography and the butchering of animals (stock footage, most likely from the 1915 *safari* film **Lady Mackenzie's Big Game Pictures**) was mixed with new shots of naked "native" women – actually local black actresses and prostitutes – horny gorillas (men in costumes), pygmies (local black children), and the outrageous central theme of human/ape miscegenation. A "mating ritual" (or rape) scene between a huge gorilla and a bare-breasted (and bald) "native" female was staged by alpha ape-impersonator Charles Gemora and a negro film extra. Naturally, the film was a huge commercial success, benefitting vastly from the "negative" publicity surrounding its lack of authenticity. Footage from **Ingagi** (and other exotic films) was recut and re-dubbed by Samuel Cummins as **Love Life Of A Gorilla** in 1937 (updated and reissued in 1940 as **Kidnapping Gorillas**)[1]. The same team responsible for the original **Ingagi** followed up with another confection of ethno-exotica, **Nu-Ma-Pu – Cannibalism**, in 1931, this

time with hijacked footage of human flesh-eaters shot in the Solomon Islands (Gemora is credited as playing one of the hungry natives in additional faked shots). A similar film of this period was **Wild Women Of Borneo** (Charles Diltz, 1931), which comprised ethnographic footage (including native nudity and walking on hot coals) from various countries; the final section, which purports to be from Borneo and shows a gaggle of naked, large-breasted "native" women cavorting in a forest, was almost certainly shot in Los Angeles (or perhaps Mexico) using movie props and local coloured prostitutes. Another 1930 production in this vein was **Mawas**, a short from producer Max Graf, with a story set in the East Indian jungle and faked scenes of an orang-utan mauling a native bearer to death, while **Ingagi**'s theme of girl-ape

sex was faintly echoed in **Ourang**, a 1930 Universal project which morphed into **East Of Borneo** (for which pre-release art showed a monstrous ape-arm dragging a blonde by the hair). As for Charles Gemora, his gorilla-act continued to be in great demand, both in dramatic features – such as Jack Conway's **The Unholy Three**[2] – and also in a number of short comedies. He appeared in the Mack Sennett comedies **Ghost Parade** (1931) – in which his head-mask is removed – **Monkey Business In Africa** (1931), and **Hawkins And Watkins, Inc** (1932, as a gorilla that hi-jacks a plane), as well as more short films for Hal Roach, including: **Sealskins** (1932), a bizarre film set in a boarding-house for circus freaks, also featuring midget Major Mite; Laurel and Hardy's strangely mistitled **The Chimp** (1932), in which he appears as a tutu-

INGAGI – THE GORILLA'S RAPE-ATTACK (*OPPOSITE PAGE*);
THE NATIVES' SPEAR-ATTACK (*ABOVE*); PRODUCTION
PHOTOGRAPHS.

wearing female ex-circus gorilla; Charley Chase's **Nature In The Wrong** (1933), as a piano-playing gorilla named Mr. Chadwick; and **Bum Voyage** (1934),[3] as a gorilla running riot on a passenger ship. Uncredited appearances from this period include roles in Universal's **Scared Stiff** (1931) – a Red Star comedy involving diamond thieves in the African jungle – Del Lord's **Gum Shoes** (1935), and Universal's feature **Oh, Doctor** (1937).[4]

1. **Kidnapping Gorillas** may have been the film released in 1946 by Dwain Esper as **Return Of Ingagi**, although some reports indicate that this roadshow item – screened in a package with **Sins Of Love** and **Facts Of Life** (a short film aimed at selling Esper's 1944 sex hygiene book of that name) – was actually the original **Ingagi** repackaged. Any link to Ben Burbidge's **Kidnapping Gorillas** is unclear.

2. This remake of Tod Browning's 1925 original is updated for sound, and retains two of Browning's main actors – Lon Chaney and midget Harry Earles – as well as its essential plotline. The main difference is in the gorilla; Browning used somewhat ridiculous blown-up shots of a chimpanzee, but here the role is ably assumed by Gemora.

3. **Bum Voyage** also features actress Patsy Kelly wearing a gorilla costume. The film was one of over twenty short farces starring Kelly and Thelma Todd, produced by Roach between 1933 and 1935; another of interest was **The Tin Man** (1935), concerning a robot and a mad scientist. **Sealskins** also featured Todd, but in her previous Roach pairing with Zasu Pitts which included seventeen films between 1931 and 1933.

4. Some of these roles may actually have been played by Clarence Morehouse, an associate or understudy of Gemora's.

THE UNHOLY THREE – PRODUCTION PHOTOGRAPHS (*OVERLEAF VERSO*).

GHOST PARADE – PRODUCTION PHOTOGRAPH (*OVERLEAF RECTO TOP*); HAWKINS AND WATKINS, INC – PRODUCTION PHOTOGRAPH (*OVERLEAF RECTO BOTTOM*).

494-77

494-88

NATURE IN THE WRONG – PRODUCTION PHOTOGRAPH (*FOLLOWING PAGES*).

SEALSKINS – PRODUCTION PHOTOGRAPH (*ABOVE*); THE
CHIMP – PRODUCTION PHOTOGRAPH (*LEFT*).

GUM SHOES – PRODUCTION PHOTOGRAPH (*ABOVE*); OH
DOCTOR – PRODUCTION PHOTOGRAPH (*RIGHT*).
BUM VOYAGE – PRODUCTION PHOTOGRAPH (*FOLLOWING
PAGES*).

EAST OF BORNEO
(George Melford, 1931: USA)

Completely devoid of comic relief, Universal's dark jungle-sex thriller stars Rose Hobart as a young white woman who takes a trip into the heart of darkness – three hundred miles upriver to Marudu, a hidden, crocodile-infested citadel in the primal Asian wilderness – to find her estranged husband, a doctor who is kept in a drunken stupor for the amusement of Hashin, a mysterious Aryan prince. **East Of Borneo** has scenes of horror (a miscreant native devoured alive by crocodiles, a sadistic nocturnal man-hunt, a bestial ape), exotic art design by Charles D. Hall, Noble Johnson as Hashin's servant, and Lupita Tovar as a love-lorn native serving-girl. Footage from **East Of Borneo** was later used in Harry Garson's **Beast Of Borneo** (1933) a jungle-horror thriller concerning a giant, homicidal orang-utan. One of the last films to be based on the monkey-human organ transplants of Dr. Serge Voronoff, which inspired several weird cine-narratives during the previous decade, **Beast Of Borneo** tracks a mad vivisectionist named Borodoff, who heads into the jungle to conduct evolutionary experiments on a live ape; the enraged beast finally crushes him to death. The orang-utan is played by a large actor in ape-costume, intercut with close-ups of an actual, mild-looking specimen.

TARZAN THE APE MAN – PRODUCTION PHOTOGRAPH.
STUNTMAN RAY CORRIGAN IS OFTEN CITED AS PLAYING THE
"FRIENDLY" APE, AND WAS ALSO ONE OF JOHNNY
WEISSMULLER'S SEVERAL STUNT STAND-INS.

TARZAN THE APE MAN – THE GORILLA-MONSTER PIT;
PRODUCTION PHOTOGRAPHS (*FOLLOWING PAGES*).

TARZAN THE APE MAN
(W.S. Van Dyke, 1931: USA)

This adaptation of the Edgar Rice Burroughs jungle fantasy, released by MGM in 1932, firmly established the character of Tarzan as a populist film icon, with its star Johnny Weissmuller repeating the role in a further eleven movies (the last six produced by RKO). *Tarzan The Ape Man*, a newspaper comic strip illustrated by Hal Foster, had already commenced publication in 1929. The film version is a prime example of pseudo-ethnography, utilising rear-projected stock footage to "recreate" Africa, while white dwarfs were shaven and painted black to portray jungle pygmies – no less than fifty dwarfs were rounded up by MGM to play a whole savage tribe, whose village is crushed by elephants. Several dwarfs were apparently trampled to pulp by the stampeding beasts on camera, adding a "freak snuff" element to proceedings. In another sequence, natives hurl themselves into a pit to be smashed by a huge gorilla (played by Jack Leonard in a sinister, monstrous ape-suit – Leonard would also impersonate a vicious gorilla in Universal's 12-chapter serial **Jungle Mystery**, released the same year, and in the comic short **Mickey's Ape Man**, released in 1933). Dwarfs had others uses, too; they were often stuffed into costumes and made to play various animals in many of the jungle films of the 30s, 40s and 50s; in **Tarzan The Ape Man**, Johnny Eck, the "half-boy" star of Tod Browning's **Freaks**, plays a grotesque bird-creature – footage which was apparently filmed during the production of **Freaks**, and which is also inserted into **Tarzan Escapes** (1936) and

TARZAN THE APE MAN – PRODUCTION PHOTOGRAPHS (*OPPOSITE PAGE*).

TARZAN AND HIS MATE – FRIENDLY APES; PRODUCTION PHOTOGRAPH (*ABOVE*).

Tarzan's Secret Treasure (1941). **Tarzan The Ape Man** was followed by **Tarzan And His Mate** (1933), complete with a barely-covered Jane (actress Maureen O'Sullivan) in frontal nude swimming scenes (actually performed by body double Josephine McKim), a crocodile attack, gangs of costume gorillas and chimps, and other frolics.[1] The film is also notable for its painted background mattes, created by Warren Newcombe. The jungle mania sparked by the release of **Tarzan The Ape Man** inevitably inspired parodies, copies, and also poverty-row variants such as Harry L. Fraser's **The Savage Girl** (1932), starring Rochelle Hudson as a white-skinned jungle-dweller with a loyal gorilla (played by Charles Gemora) which brutally kills a would-be rapist when she is captured by hunters. Produced by Monarch, and supervised by Burton King, **The Savage Girl** was actually retitled **La Mujer Tarzan** ("The Female Tarzan") for its later Mexican release. Another jungle girl appeared in the crude 1-reel Terrytoon animation **Farmer Alfalfa's Ape Girl** (also 1932); the cartoon was notable for its daring depictions of the girl's nude buttocks in various situations. And in the RKO 2-reel farce **Thru Thin And Thicket, or Who's Zoo In Africa** (also 1932), a "female Tarzan" is the object of ridicule.

1. There were also shots of bare-breasted "native" females, which were presumably cut for most screenings. Jane's nude swim was reportedly filmed and used in various states of undress, ranging from totally covered to totally naked.

THE MURDERS IN THE RUE MORGUE – PRODUCTION
PHOTOGRAPHS (*THIS PAGE, OPPOSITE & FOLLOWING PAGES*).

The MURDERS IN THE RUE MORGUE

(Robert Florey, 1931: USA)

Universal's third major sound horror film used Edgar Allan Poe as its source material, making this the first major studio adaptation of that writer, although not much of Poe's original detective story remains. Released in 1932, the film starred Bela Lugosi in the first of three films which used Poe in this way, discarding most of the plot but retaining the title as an attraction (the other two films were **The Black Cat** and **The Raven**). In **Murders In The Rue Morgue**, Lugosi plays showman Dr. Mirakle, whose prize exhibit is Erik, a freakish, depraved ape (played by Charles Gemora in his gorilla suit, doubled in some scenes by Joe Bonomo).[1] Mirakle secretly kidnaps girls to use in weird evolutionary experiments involving the ape, resulting in their deaths. As this implies, bestial miscegeny is the scientist's ultimate objective. Scenes include the torture and crucifixion of a prostitute – rejected as Erik's mate due to her syphilitic blood – and it's believed that the film's relatively short running time may be due to similarly sadistic sequences being excised by Universal. Nonetheless, it retains a disturbing sequence in which Camille, a virgin chosen by Mirakle for her "pure blood", is seemingly raped by the rampaging ape. As directed by Robert Florey, designed by Charles D. Hall and photographed by Karl Freund, the film achieves a

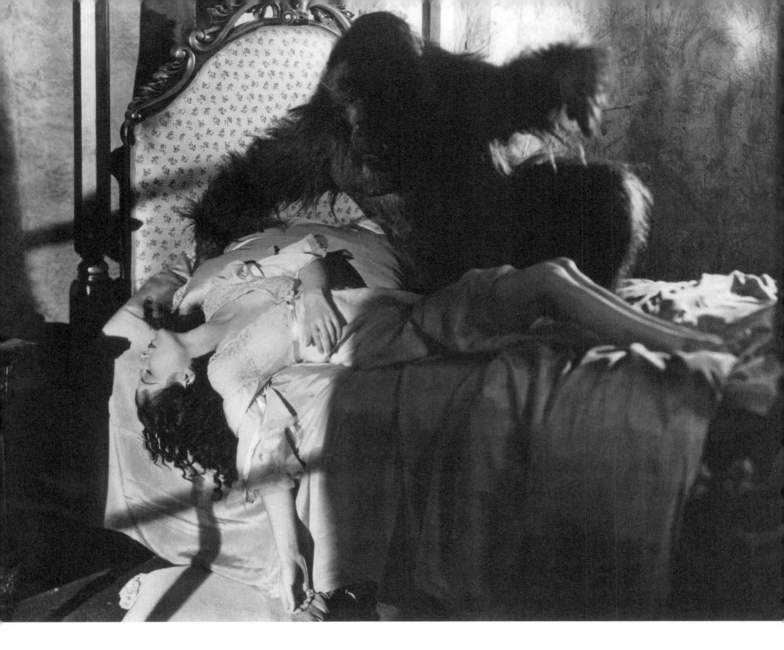

grotesque ambience of physical and mental distortion, propelled by relentless camera-work, and with Lugosi's electric performance as the madman at its epicentre. The film is spoiled only by ridiculous sequences in which Gemora's gorilla-monster is replaced, inexplicably, with close-ups of a chimp. Director Florey's only notable return to the horror genre was **The Beast With Five Fingers** (1946). Poe had followed his story "The Murders In The Rue Morgue" with a sequel, "The Mystery Of Marie Rogêt", written in 1842; based on the unsolved murder of a young girl, Mary Rogers, in New York, it was perhaps the first story of its kind to be based on a real-life homicide. A century later, Universal followed up their **Murders In The Rue Morgue** with a film adaptation, the first, of Poe's sequel. **The Mystery Of Marie Roget** (1942), which featured Maria Montez in short scenes as the murdered girl, was framed as a gothic mystery tale; when Montez became famous, Realart gave her star billing in a re-release entitled **Phantom Of Paris**, with the tag-line: "HER FACE DESTROYED BY THE PHANTOM MANGLER – ONLY A BEAST COULD COMMIT SUCH A CRIME!".

1. Gemora can also be seen, briefly, as a caged gorilla in the opening sequences of another classic horror movie of this period, Island Of Lost Souls (1932).

THE HORROR – LOBBY CARD.

The HORROR
(Bud Pollard, 1932: USA)

Perhaps inspired by Adam Hull Shirk's stage-play *The Ape*, **The Horror** is an extremely strange, seldom-seen horror/mystery movie shot in 5 days by base-level director Pollard. The story revolves around the theft of a Hindu treasure by an explorer, who subsequently suffers guilt and nightmares – one of which forms the film's main events. One night, the man is assailed in his mansion by a sinister Indian mystic (played by stage illusionist Raja Raboid), who brings with him a dwarfish assistant, a gorilla and a snake, which attacks and bites his wife (played by snake dancer/stripper Nyreda Montez). The man is also trampled by the huge ape, and then ses his face transform into that of a monstrous beast, a mutation caused by the mystic's curse. When morning finally comes, the jewel-thief has been reduced to a gibbering lunatic. A Japanese version of **The Horror**, entitled **Jumen** ("Beast-Face"), was released in May 1935 by Daito Shoji. The film was re-edited by Pollard in the 1940s and turned into a 40-minute anti-alcohol film entitled **John The Drunkard**, with the original horror scenes now doubling as hideous drink-fuelled hallucinations.

The INTRUDER
(Albert Ray, 1932: USA)

During this period of multiple mystery films with weird narrative devices, few can compare for sheer audacity to **The Intruder** (also known as **Horror In The Night**), an Allied Pictures zero-budget night-trip. The film opens on a storm-blasted cruise ship, the *S.S. Intruder*, where a bloody axe-murder has just been perpetrated. Confusion and panic escalate as the ship starts sinking – shown by blatantly synthetic model-work – and the film then morphs into a strange island adventure. The group of ship-wrecked survivors – one the killer – are haunted by bizarre sounds and shadows, and soon encounter a jungle wild-man (played by Mischa Auer), his lumbering gorilla (which shrieks like a bird), and a cave full of skeletons. Eventually the murder is solved and the survivors – including the wild man, accompanied by a female skeleton called Mary – are rescued by a French vessel.

CREATION CONCEPT PAINTING FOR A GIANT GORILLA FILM; ART BY WILLIS O'BRIEN AND BYRON CRABBE, c.1931.

KING KONG
(Merian C. Cooper & Ernest B. Schoedsack, 1932-33: USA)

Following the success of director Harry O. Hoyt and animator Willis O'Brien's stop-motion dinosaur fantasy **The Lost World** in 1925, RKO hired the pair to recreate and improve the film's basic format for the new sound era. The result of this fresh collaboration was **Creation**, a scenario in which a group of sub-mariners and ship-wrecked civilians, caught up in a colossal tempest at sea, emerge in a volcanic lake on an uncharted island. They soon discover that this island is inhabited by dinosaurs

KING KONG – CONCEPT PRODUCTION ART BY MARIO LARRINAGA (*OPPOSITE*); PRODUCTION PHOTOGRAPHS (*ABOVE & FOLLOWING PAGES*).

and other prehistoric creatures. Producer Merian C. Cooper halted production of the film after the shooting of just two sequences, citing mounting costs and doubts concerning commercial viability; but out of the project's extensive pre-production work, which included new ways of rendering glass mattes, live action and animation, he saw enough to inspire him into a new envisioning of the plot – the story was re-written, merging into an idea which Cooper had conceived around gorillas battling giant lizards. Mystery writer Edgar Wallace produced the first draft of a script, entitled *The Beast*, but died before he could revise it; several months later, *The Beast* had become **King Kong**. Cooper and long-time colleague Schoedsack – the pair became involved in ethnographic film-making in the early 1920s as part of Captain Edward Salisbury's extensive South Pacific expeditions, shooting footage which ended up in such exotic documentaries as **Gow The Head Hunter** (1928) and **Ra-Mu: Children Of The Sun** (1929) – formulated the story of Skull Island, a forbidden zone in the cruel South Seas where, behind the walls of a massive jungle fortress, natives make human sacrifices to Kong, an enormous prehistoric ape. This massive project took nearly two years to film, and lead actress Fay Wray – playing the giant ape's blonde and unlikely love interest – was doubled by at least eight different stuntgirls, including Aline Goodwin, Lillian Jones, Lee Kinney, Judy Malcolm, Cherie May, Pauline Wagner, Marcella Allen, and Loretta Rush (whose history of daring stunts included diving into a lake of burning gasoline in **Flowing Gold**, in 1924). With special effects by O'Brien – many deriving from his uncompleted work on **Creation** – **King Kong** became a box-office sensation and one of the all-time classic fantasy movies. It also contained a number of controversial scenes deemed too strong for post-Code audiences – when the film was re-released in 1938, studio censors cut various "shocking"sequences, including: natives and others being crushed in Kong's mouth or trampled into the mud; a woman being snatched from her New York apartment and hurled to her death far below; and a scene of Kong peeling away Fay Wray's clothing (an almost subliminal insert of Wray baring her breasts in a nude swimming scene remained). Legend also tells of a filmed but then removed (before release) "spider-pit" sequence featuring giant man-eating arachnids and other crawling horrors, but no footage has been located. It has been surmised that RKO may have been encouraged to produce **King Kong** after the commercial success of **Ingagi** (1930), the independent jungle-ape feature which they picked up for distribution. Ernest B. Schoedsack and RKO made a sequel to **King Kong**, entitled **Son Of Kong**, in 1933, in which expedition leader Carl Denham returns to Skull

SON OF KONG – PRODUCTION PHOTOGRAPH (*ABOVE*).
THE LOST ISLAND – CHARLES GEMORA AS KONG, WITH
MAE WEST DOLL; PRODUCTION PHOTOGRAPH (*LEFT*).

Island and discovers the mighty ape's pale-furred, orphaned offspring; Willis O'Brien again contributed special effects, but overall the film is far lighter and less substantial than the original. (O'Brien was also struck by personal tragedy during production, when his estranged and terminally ill wife shot and killed their two sons, before turning the gun on herself.) An abandoned Kong-related project, dating from 1934, was **The New Adventures Of King Kong**, conceived by Cooper, depicting the voyage from Skull Island back to New York. During the voyage, the ship is assailed by monsters and Kong is unchained to battle them; Schoedsack ultimately rejected the idea, and it was never advanced.[1] Schoedsack and O'Brien finally teamed up once again to produce **Mighty Joe Young** (1949), a scaled-down re-imagining of the Kong story, this time featuring an over-sized African beast.[2]

1. Perhaps the most unusual film to emerge in **King Kong**'s wake was the uncompleted **The Lost Island** (LeRoy Prinz, 1934), conceived as a bizarre Technicolor parody in which the giant gorilla (played by Charles Gemora) interacts with a dinosaur (another man in a suit) and a range of marionettes, all modelled on contemporary Hollywood stars (the blonde puppet of Ann Darrow, Kong's bride, was reportedly based on Mae West). Lack of funding is cited as the reason for non-completion of the movie, which promised to be one of the strangest ever made.

2. O'Brien seemingly worked on new King Kong ideas and projects until the end of his life (he died in 1962); as late as 1960 he created oil painting concept art for a film entitled **King Kong Vs. Frankenstein**; the film was never made, but the idea possibly inspired the Toho production **Kingu Kongu Tai Gojira** (1962).

JUNGLE MYSTERY
(Ray Taylor, 1931-32: USA)

A 12-chapter serial based on Talbot Mundy's *Ivory Trail*, a 1918 collection of exotic adventure stories set in British East Africa, and directed by Ray Taylor, who during the 1930s oversaw many of Universal's more bizarre serials. Tom Tyler takes the leading role, and hulking actor Sam Baker features as Zungu, a weird half-ape, half-human hybrid; Baker also appeared as "Gwana" in the Paramount feature **King Of The Jungle**, made that same year. The twelve chapters of **Jungle Mystery** were: **Into The Dark Continent**; **The Ivory Trail**; **The Death Stream**; **Poisoned Fangs**; **The Mystery Cavern**; **Daylight Doom**; **The Jaws Of Death**; **Trapped By The Enemy**; **The Jungle Terror**; **Ambushed!**; **The Lion's Fury**; and **Buried Treasure**. The serial was released during the height of Hollywood's "jungle fever", prompted by the success of such films as **Trader Horn** and **Tarzan The Ape Man**.

FORBIDDEN ADVENTURE
(J.C. Cook, 1934: USA)

Produced by Dwain Esper's Road Show Attractions, **Forbidden Adventure** is one of the most crudely assembled and maniacal of all the 30s "jungle adventure" movies that were created primarily to display film footage of naked "native" women and savage animal attacks. It is also notable as a particularly exploitational entry in the "white jungle queen" genre. The story concerns two white explorers in Borneo, who discover a lost tribe ruled by a nubile white girl. She tells them that she is a Russian girl named Ileana, that her father was murdered when she was a child, and her mother repeatedly raped until she was driven insane. Finally the mother and child were abandoned in the jungle. The mother gained revenge on her rapist by hypnotizing jungle beasts and commanding them to tear him apart. Then they were discovered by the tribe, who now worship Ileana as a goddess. Finally the deranged old woman perishes in a fire, and Ileana is free to return to civilization. With its stock footage and exploitational images of nude "savages" sutured roughly together, overdubbed and spliced with new shots of the "whites" and the disturbing madwoman, **Forbidden Adventure** is another prime construct of hallucinatory trash from the great Esper; it was reissued in 1936 by J.H. Hoffberg as **Inyaah, Jungle Goddess**, and again by Esper's Mapel Attractions under various titles, including **Strange Adventures, Jungle Virgin** and **The Virgin Of Sarawak**.

THE SIGN OF THE CROSS – APE-RAPE IN THE ROMAN ARENA; PRODUCTION PHOTOGRAPH (*OPPOSITE*).

The SIGN OF THE CROSS
(Cecil B. DeMille, 1932: USA)

After the furore surrounding Tod Browning's **Freaks**, film-makers became, for a while at least, more sensitive to the issue of employing real human anomalies in their productions. This is reputedly why Cecil B. DeMille withdrew from his Roman epic **The Sign Of The Cross** an undoubtedly outlandish sequence depicting vicious, half-naked female gladiators fighting achondroplasic dwarfs in the Roman arena (scenes in which **Freaks** star Angelo Rossitto played a pygmy who is brutally impaled). This classic example of freak cinema has now, thankfully, been restored. DeMille was still able to present such scenes as a blonde (said to be Ruth Clifford) chained naked to a statue of Pan and about to be raped by a priapic ape (played by Charles Gemora), corpses piled on carts, victims trampled and gored by elephants or devoured alive by alligators (including erotic dancer Sally Rand and a scene performed by Joe Bonomo which was deemed to gruesome for the final cut), martyred saints, a seductive orgy scene with temple-girl Ancaria (Joyzelle Joyner)[1] performing the lesbo-erotic "Dance of the Naked Moon", and a nude Claudette Colbert bathing in milk; these sado-erotic flourishes, coupled with the film's seminal historic subject – the Emperor Nero's systematic butchering and burning of the Christian scum – make **The Sign Of The Cross** the most transgressive of all the American costume epics.

SO THIS IS AFRICA
(Edward F. Cline, 1932: USA)

A legendary sex-farce from Columbia Pictures, said by some to be the most outrageous artifact to be brazenly submitted for certification in the annals of pre-Code cinema. It was rejected with extreme prejudice by the censor board, who would only permit its exhibition in 1933 after an estimated 1,500 feet – equivalent to around one third of its original running time – had been brutally hacked out, excising whole swathes of dialogue clotted with sexual innunendo, scenes swirling with semi-nudity and lust, and other transgressions considered irremediably beyond the pale. It was never re-released. Heralded by tag-lines such as "Two sexplorers go big dame hunting in Africa!", **So This is Africa** was the only non-RKO film made by sleazy comedic duo Wheeler and Woolsey – ex-vaudeville clowns, one of them perpetually sucking in desperation on a penis-substitute cigar – who began in the silent era. Travelling to Africa in search of work, the duo find themselves at the mercy of various sexual predators, including a libidinous female explorer, an amorous she-gorilla (played by Clarence Morehouse, said to be a close associate of Charles Gemora), and a tribe of nymphomaniac Amazons who threaten to kill them with erotic exhaustion.[1] Dressing in drag to avoid the latter fate, the doomed pair are instead swept off by jungle-men in a yearly mating ceremony. The film closes with one year later, with scenes of the two transvestites resigned to their fate as jungle brides, presumably after enduring twelve months of remorseless passive sodomy.[2] Clarence Morehouse's other gorilla-suit credits include the short comedy **Pure And Simple** (1930), causing havoc among a group of ship-wrecked show-girls, and he was also said to feature in the notorious **Ingagi**, perhaps alternating with Charles Gemora. Jack Leonard was the gorilla-impersonator in Wheeler and Woolsey's **Diplomaniacs** (1933).

1. So This Is Africa saw a film debut by 15-year-old Patricia Douglas as an Amazon dancer; a few years later, in 1937, Douglas would file an unprecedented prosecution against MGM, after she was allegedly brutally raped at an orgiastic studio stag party.

2. So This Is Africa may well have been part-inspired by Mack Sennett's earlier **Monkey Business In Africa** (1931), in which an intrepid pair venture to Africa to make a film entitled "Gorilla Love" and end up in gorilla costumes surrounded by real gorillas (which are of course in reality other men in gorilla suits, including leading ape impersonator Charles Gemora). Both films could have inspired the 1938 comedy **Three Missing Links**, one of the first films by inane comic trio the Three Stooges, who were launched by Columbia in 1934 with **Woman Haters**. Another jungle comedy with gorillas (and Gemora) was Universal's **The Cohens And The Kellys in Africa** (1930).

SO THIS IS AFRICA – PRODUCTION PHOTOGRAPH (*OVERLEAF VERSO*).

THREE MISSING LINKS – RAY CORRIGAN (BILLED AS NABA, A GORILLA); PRODUCTION PHOTOGRAPH (*OVERLEAF RECTO TOP*); THE COHENS AND THE KELLYS IN AFRICA – PRODUCTION PHOTOGRAPH (*OVERLEAF RECTO BOTTOM*).

TARZAN THE FEARLESS

(Robert F. Hill, 1932: USA)

Filmed around the same time as **Tarzan The Ape Man**, but not released until 1933 due to a financial arrangement with MGM, Sol Lesser's 12-chapter serial **Tarzan The Fearless** starred Buster Crabbe, who had just played "Kaspa the Lion Man", an obvious Tarzan copy, in Paramount's **King Of The Jungle** (1932). Compared to the MGM film, Lesser's serial is a cheap work of pulp cinema, revelling in images of a lost civilization ruled by a malevolent High Priest (played by Mischa Auer), human sacrifices to the pagan idol Zar (borrowed from Universal's **The Mummy**), human bone pits, voodoo rites, a were-tiger killed by a silver bullet, man-eating plants, and a rampaging homicidal gorilla, Bolgani (most likely played by Jack Leonard)[1]. Lead actress Jacqueline Wells also revealed plenty of flesh in a skimpy jungle costume. Lesser devised a new and original format for the films' release, a marketing device he called the "feature-serial" – the first four chapters were edited into a single 70-minute feature, to be followed by the remaining eight weekly episodes. Later, the feature and the final episode were also edited together to make yet another version, running at around 85 minutes. The chapters of **Tarzan The Fearless** were: **The Dive Of Death; The Storm God Strikes; Thundering Death; The Pit Of Peril; Blood Money; Voodoo Vengeance; Caught By Cannibals; The Creeping Terror; Eyes Of Evil; The Death Plunge; Harvest Of Hate;** and **Jungle Justice**.

EYES OF EVIL – SCENE FROM CHAPTER 9 OF **TARZAN THE FEARLESS**, WITH JACK LEONARD AS GORILLA; PRODUCTION PHOTOGRAPH FROM PRINTED LOBBY CARD.

TOM TYLER'S LUCK – PRODUCTION PHOTOGRAPH (*OVERLEAF VERSO*).

1. Another of Jack Leonard's major gorilla roles was in Universal's 12-chapter jungle serial **Tim Tyler's Luck** (1937), directed by Ford Beebe and Wyndham Gittens and based on a 1928 King Features adventure comic strip by Lyman Young. Set in Africa, the plot sees Tyler pitched against his nemesis, Spider Webb. Another famous ape-impersonator, Charles Gemora, also appears, with both gorillas featuring in some scenes. The serial's chapters were: **Jungle Pirates**; **Dead Man's Pass**; **Into The Lion's Den**; **The Ivory Trail**; **Trapped In The Quicksands**; **The Jaws Of The Jungle**; **The King Of The Gorillas**; **The Spider Caught**; **The Gates Of Doom**; **A Race For Fortune**; **No Man's Land**; and **The Kimberley Diamonds**. Universal also produced another jungle serial in 1937 – **Jungle Jim**, based on Alex Raymond-drawn comic character of the same name. It was directed by Ford Beebe and Clifford Smith in twelve chapters, which were: **Into The Lion's Den**; **The Cobra Strikes**; **The Menacing Hand**; **The Killer's Trail**; **The Bridge Of Terror**; **Drums Of Doom**; **The Earth Trembles**; **The Killer Lion**; **The Devil Bird**; **Descending Doom**; **In The Cobra's Castle**; and **The Last Safari**. The plot revolved around the already standard genre trope of a white-skinned heiress lost in the jungle. Raymond started the *Jungle Jim* strip in 1934, reputedly as a deliberate attempt by King Features to rival the popularity of *Tarzan*, which was published by United Feature Syndicate. In 1948, Sam Katzman hired Johnny Weissmuller – whose final film as Tarzan was **Tarzan And The Mermaids**, released that same year – to play Jim in a series of low-budget pulp adventures, often featuring black-painted dwarfs, men in gorilla-suits, blondes in leopard-skin bikinis, and other staples of 1940s/50s jungle trash cinema. Jack Leonard's final gorilla outing came in Columbia's 15-chapter serial **Terry And The Pirates** (1940), based on the comic strip by Milton Caniff. Set in the Asian jungle, the serial involves the quest for a lost city and a pirate gang known as the Tiger Men, as well as Leonard's strangely misplaced beast. The fifteen chapters were: **Into The Great Unknown**; **The Fang Strikes**; **The Mountain Of Death**; **The Dragon Queen Threatens**; **At The Mercy Of The Mob**; **The Scroll Of Wealth**; **Angry Waters**; **The Tomb Of Peril**; **Jungle Hurricane**; **Too Many Enemies**; **Walls Of Doom**; **No Escape**; **The Fatal Mistake**; **Pyre Of Death**; and **The Secret Of The Temple**.

BLONDE VENUS – "HOT VOODOO"; PRODUCTION PHOTOGRAPH.

BLONDE VENUS
(Josef von Sternberg, 1932: USA)
One of cinema's most bizarre dance segments of 1932 comes from **Blonde Venus**, when Marlene Dietrich, initially dressed in a gorilla-suit, performs the exotic cabaret number "Hot Voodoo" to a background of tribal drumming and painted savages (presumably reflecting the African origins of *vaudou*).

WRONGORILLA
(Alfred J. Goulding, 1933: USA)
In an era when Hollywood comedy shorts often parodied the feature-film hits of the day, **Wrongorilla** was a cash-in on Martin and Osa Johnson's 1932 jungle documentary **Congorilla**. Produced by Vitaphone, **Wrongorilla** starred Jack Haley and was set in a circus sideshow, where an escaped gorilla causes havoc. The gorilla-man who plaed the ape is not creditted.

WASEI KINGU KONGU – PRODUCTION PHOTOGRAPH
(ABOVE).
KINGU KONGU – PRODUCTION PHOTOGRAPHS (*OPPOSITE*).

WASEI KINGU KONGU

("Japanese-Made King Kong"; Torajiro Saito, 1933: Japan)

The global success of RKO's **King Kong** led not only to a quick sequel, but also to blatant cash-ins; in Japan, for example, the film's popularity – and that of its sequel, **Son Of Kong**, which was released by Shochiku in 1935 under the title **Kongu No Fukushu** ("Revenge Of Kong") – inspired a bizarre tribute, **Wasei Kingu Kongu**, from Shochiku Kinema. Actor Isamu Yamaguchi, a "heavy" in numerous movies, played a man playing Kong in a gorilla-suit, as part of a stage-act inspired by the RKO movie. When he jumps off-stage in costume to pursue an enemy through the streets, chaos ensues. A few years later, low-budget company Zensho Kinema released Soya Kumagai's 2-part **Kingu Kongu** (1938), less giant ape movie than crazed killer ape movie, involving a kidnapper with a trained gorilla-man creature (played by Ryunosuke Kabayama) and a disfigured, hunchbacked henchman. This film is also known as **Edo Ni Arawareta Kingu Kongu** ("King Kong Appears In Edo"). Even in the late 1930s, Zensho productions were released as silent movies with recorded commentary soundtracks, due to budget restraints. Also in 1938, Daito Eiga contributed a *pannikku komedi* ("panic comedy") entitled **Mitsurin No Kaiju-Gun** ("Secret Jungle Monster Group") to the sub-Kong genre; directed by Toshihide Amauchi, this absurdist adventure involved college students who encounter a race of deranged sub-anthropoids in the Chichibu mountains.

HOUSE OF MYSTERY
(William Nigh, 1934: USA)
Based on *The Ape*, a 1926 mystery play by Adam Hull Shirk – who also provided the story for gorilla-nudie classic **Ingagi** – **House Of Mystery** is an old dark house thriller from Monogram, which features a homicidal gorilla, Hindu curses, and phoney séances. In the film's prologue, an archaeologist in India is cursed by Kali-temple priests when he kills a sacred monkey, steals treasures, and absconds with Chanda, a holy dancing-girl (played by Joyzelle Joyner). Twenty years later in America, the curse is manifested in the form of a huge, neck-snapping gorilla-monster, which stalks the occupants of the doomed man's mansion under Chanda's secret control. She finally proves to be a servant of Kali, and completes the sect's vengeance. The identity of the actor who wore the gorilla costume is not recorded, but some speculate that it may constitute the first film appearance by ape-impersonator Emil van Horn, who that year appeared as a gorilla in a 1-act stage sketch entitled *Murder At Midnight*. Monogram credited Shirk's play as an inspiration once more in 1940, when concocting the Karloff horror vehicle **The Ape**, although the films' plots are totally different.

The LOST JUNGLE
(David Howard & Armand Schaefer, 1934: USA)
A 12-chapter Mascot jungle serial starring Clyde Beatty, the whip-wielding circus lion-tamer whose speciality seems to have been staging fights between lions and tigers – encounters from which the lion almost always emerged victorious. At least one such death-fight was contrived for the cameras during the filming of his debut feature movie, **The Big Cage** (Universal, 1933), resulting in the bloody and fatal mangling of a Bengal tiger. Beatty was himself severely mauled in 1932 by a massive lion named Nero, which dragged him around its cage by his leg. At this point his big cat act consisted of around forty beasts, both lions and tigers mixed together in one ringed steel enclosure. The success of **The Big Cage** led to Beatty's starring role in **The Lost Jungle**, whose twelve chapters were: **Noah's Ark Island; Nature In The Raw; The Hypnotic Eye; The Pit Of Crocodiles; Gorilla Warfare; The Battle Of Beasts; The Tiger's Prey; The Lion's Brood; Eyes Of The Jungle; Human Hyenas; The Gorilla;** and **Take Them Back Alive.** Some of the best scenes are set in the "buried city" of Kamor, featuring actor Frank Lanning as a jungle wild man, a pit of man-eating

THE LOST JUNGLE – PRODUCTION PHOTOGRAPH.

crocodiles, and a bloodthirsty gorilla (seemingly played by Charles Gemora). Real animals were provided by the Hagenbeck-Wallace zoo. The serial was also released simultaneously as a 7-reel feature, apparently with significant amounts of previously unused footage.

BRING 'EM BACK A LIE – PRODUCTION PHOTOGRAPH.

BRING 'EM BACK A LIE
(Alfred J. Goulding, 1935: USA)
The success of Frank Buck's 1931 jungle adventure movie **Bring 'Em Back Alive** soon spawned a full quota of parody shorts, including Mack Sennett's **Bring 'Em Back Sober**, starring famous film lion Jackie. Buck's film was even invoked by an underground nudie-stag reel, entitled **Bring 'Em Back Nude** and featuring an erotic jungle scenario of naked white girls and a gorilla. Another short comedy in this sub-genre was **Bring 'Em Back A Lie** (1935), starring not only Ben Turpin but two of Hollywood's leading gorilla impersonators, Jack Leonard and Ray "Crash" Corrigan, and featuring bizarre laboratory experiments with Strickfaden electricity machines. **Frank Duck Brings 'Em Back Alive** (1946) was a belated cartoon parody from Disney, with their character Donald Duck (created in 1934) as the hunter.

CHARLIE CHAN AT THE CIRCUS – PRODUCTION
PHOTOGRAPH.

CHARLIE CHAN AT THE CIRCUS
(Harry Lachman, 1936: USA)

In 1931 the role of Charlie Chan, Chinese-American detective, was assigned to actor Warner Oland – presumably due to his successful impersonation of Oriental supervillain Fu Manchu in three Paramount films – starting with **Charlie Chan Carries On**, which was also made in a Spanish-language version, **Eran Trece** ("There Were Thirteen"), with actor Manuel Arbó as the detective. The next in the seres, **The Black Camel** (1931), featured Bela Lugosi as a turban-wearing mystic. **Charlie Chan's Secret** (1936) was notable for including séance scenes set in a spooky mansion, with gothic decor by art director Duncan Kramer, and cinematography by Rudolph Maté. Another Chan film of interest was **Charlie Chan At The Circus** (1936), which featured midget dancers George and Olive Brasno, giant John Aasen, and ape impersonator Charles Gemora as both Caesar, a gorilla, and as a snake-charmer impersonating Caesar (the snake-charmer was Gemora when ape-suited, J. Carrol Naish when not). Warner Oland died and was replaced by Sidney Toler as Chan in 1938; the last Fox movie was **Castle In The Desert** (1942) which, like several other entries such as **Charlie Chan At The Wax Museum** (1940), contains elements of horror movie iconography. After that the series was taken over by low-budget company Monogram, ending in 1949; actor Roland Winters replaced Toler in 1947.

DARKEST AFRICA
(B. Reeves Eason & Joseph Kane, 1936: USA)

The first pulp serial from Republic Pictures, formed in 1935 by a forced merger of six smaller poverty row studios – Monogram Pictures, Mascot Pictures, Liberty Pictures, Majestic Pictures, Chesterfield Pictures and Invincible Pictures. Partly inspired by star Clyde Beatty's earlier Mascot serial **The Lost Jungle**, the 15-chapter **Darkest Africa** was a far more lavish and bizarre production, telling the story of explorer Beatty (playing himself) discovering a vast lost city in the heart of the jungle. The city is guarded by a weird race of Bat-Men, who resemble winged Roman soldiers. The story also includes Tiger Men, a jungle boy, an ape named Bonga (played by Ray "Crash" Corrigan), and a coon character named Hambone. As with most Republic serials, stunt co-ordination was by Yakima Canutt, king of the early Hollywood stuntmen. The serial's chapters were: **Baru – Son Of The Jungle; The Tiger-Men's God; Bat-Men Of Joba; The Hunter Lions Of Joba; Bonga's Courage; Prisoners Of The High Priest; Swing For Life; Fang And Claw; When Birdmen Strike; Trial By Thunder-Rods; Jars Of Death; Revolt Of The Slaves; Gauntlet Of Destruction; The Divine Sacrifice;** and **The Prophecy Of Gorn**. It was re-released in 1948 as **King Of Jungleland**, and was later edited and condensed into the 1966 television feature **Batmen Of Africa** – one of twenty-six Republic serials sold and re-edited for television that year under the package title Century 66, all with 100-minute running times. Ray Corrigan, also featured in the classic 1936 serial **Flash Gordon** as the Orangapoid, a bizarre creature which he effected by customizing one of his gorilla costumes with a unicorn-like horn.

FORBIDDEN ADVENTURE – PRODUCTION PHOTOGRAPH.

FORBIDDEN ADVENTURE IN ANGKOR
(George M. Merrick, 1937: USA)

Made to cash in on the success of **Ingagi** (1930) and **Forbidden Adventure** (1934), this near-copy was created by acquiring **Angkor** (1935) – a British travelogue also known as **Beyond Shanghai** – and inserting new, exploitational footage including female nudity. The resulting edit purports to have been filmed at the "ancient ruins of Indo-China", and to contain actual film of the fabled "missing link" between man and ape. Its marketing sales pitch promised "orgies with wild women" – footage mainly shot in Los Angeles with local black prostitutes stripped naked for the camera, and spliced into a mélange of stock jungle footage, rear-projected travelogue slides, and scenes with actors and a man in a gorilla-suit. A tiger-attack on a female native is also included. The film was copyrighted under the title **Angkor, or Forbidden Adventure**, released in 1937 (by Dwain Esper's Roadshow Attractions) and re-released in 1938 (by Sonney Roadshow Attractions)[1] as **Forbidden Adventure**, and re-released again (by United Screen Associates) as **Gorilla Woman**. **Forbidden Adventure In Angkor** remains a prime example of pseudo-ethnographic exploitation cinema.

LOVE LIFE OF A GORILLA

(Samuel Cummins, 1937: USA)

Perhaps inflamed by the success of **Ingagi** and **Forbidden Adventure** – not to mention the public's continuing fascination with gorillas[1] – exploitation master Cummins evidently decided to construct (his credits read "assembled and edited by") a new, 6-reel Jewel production which would fuse **Ingagi** with other footage into a new visual vortex of ape-rape, miscegeny and jungle mania. Large amounts of stock footage were used, showing various wild beasts and also images of both "plate-lipped" Ubangi natives and black dwarfs of the Ituri. Although copies of the film are not freely in circulation, Cummins' promotional efforts reveal a central narrative of gorillas copulating with human females – a white-skinned female, in fact, is clearly depicted on one poster. Another poster claimed that "scientists have pondered on what might happen if gorilla and human were mated, but attempted experiments were stopped", and that "gorillas often carry off women, guard them jealously... sometimes pull their finger and toe-nails out". This poster also reproduces a photograph taken from **La Croisière Noire**, a 1926 French "cine-zoological" film, suggesting that Cummins may have culled footage of nude native girls from at least one old film travelogue. In another typical marketing ploy, Cummins also hired gorilla impersonator Emil Van Horn and stripper Zorine to perform their "beauty vs beast" act live on stage before screenings.[2] In 1940, Cummins decided to resurrect, and possibly enhance, **Love Life Of A Gorilla** under the new guise of **Kidnapping Gorillas**, with posters which clearly illustrated a scene from **Ingagi** whilst pushing the "missing link" angle of creatures half-ape and half-human.

1. Initial releases played against a real-life news back-drop concerning the capture and skeletonization of the "world's largest gorilla" by hunter/explorer George Vanderbilt; the bones of this West African beast were shipped back to the Academy of Natural Sciences in Philadelphia, where a life-like reconstruction of the creature was achieved through a new technique combining taxidermy and sculpture.

EMIL VAN HORN IN "BEAUTY AND THE BEAST", WITH DORIS HOUCK, c.1938 – PUBLICITY PHOTOGRAPHS (*LEFT &* *OPPOSITE TOP*).
EMIL VAN HORN WITH KAROL BORJA, c.1949 – PUBLICITY PHOTOGRAPH (*OPPOSITE BOTTOM*).

2. Van Horn also made performances to promote films such as **Jaws Of The Jungle** and **Dark Rapture**. Before his appearances in 1940s B-movies and serials, Van Horn – one of the most enigmatic of the Hollywood ape impersonators – had a long-running stage show in which he posed as "Ingagi, the Hollywood Gorilla" (although the ape in the original film **Ingagi** was actually Charles Gemora), assisted by Zorine as his semi-nude victim. Zorine had played Queen of the Nudists, conducting daily sacrificial rites to the Sun God, at California's 1935-36 Pacific International Exposition in San Diego, where show-entrepreneur Nate Eagle supplemented his usual midget village with Zoro Gardens, a controversial colony of (nearly) naked men and women. Van Horn and Zorine then started a popular roadshow act, whose numbers included "Beast Of The Temple" and "Death Of The Virgins". Photographs of their act from the touring *French Casino Brevities* burlesque revue of 1938 confirm that topless nudity was involved. It is not known if any of these numbers were filmed; however, a similar act from the early 1950s was recorded and released by George Weiss' Screen Classics under the title **Gorilla And The Maiden** (1953). Van Horn's act of this period – with new, younger female partner Karol Borja – was entitled "Gorilla And The Maidens", but the Screen Classics short clearly features another couple.

AT THE CIRCUS

(Edward Buzzell, 1939: USA)

The Marx Brothers – Groucho, Harpo, Chico, and Zeppo – were greatly revered by Surrealists such as Salvador Dalí, who went to Hollywood in search of Harpo Marx in 1937, and Antonin Artaud who described their work as "a kind of boiling anarchy, a kind of disintegration of the essence of the real by poetry". Although the films they made for MGM generally pale beside their earlier cinematic work, **At The Circus** (1939) at least boasts a significant quotient of sideshow shivers by the inclusion of a shambling gorilla-monster (Charles Gemora), as well as dwarf actor Jerry Maren.

THE APE – PRODUCTION PHOTOGRAPH .

The APE

(William Nigh, 1940: USA)

Boris Karloff's sixth and final film of a deal with Monogram which saw him play detective James Lee Wong on five occasions (a series based on mystery stories by Hugh Wiley published in *Colliers Magazine* from 1934 to 1938). Scripted by Curt Siodmak, **The Ape** is an early entry in the "human medical experiment" genre which prevailed in 1940s B-movie horror. Karloff plays a doctor who is desperate to cure a young woman of polio. When an escaped, homicidal circus gorilla crashes into his laboratory, he manages to kill the beast and in doing so is inspired to pursue a new treatment, the injection of human spinal fluid. Clearly deranged, the doctor decides that to procure the fluid he needs he will first flay the gorilla, then disguise himself in its skin in order to abduct and murder human donors. The ape – and presumably the doctor when dressed as an ape – were played by Ray "Crash" Corrigan who, true to custom, was billed as Nabu, giving the impression that the role was played by a real-life trained gorilla. Corrigan's next ape film was **The Strange Case Of Dr. Rx** (1942). This time billed as Nbongo, Corrigan augments his usual costume with a chain through the nose;[1] his sequences in the film – in which a hooded, mad and murderous doctor (played by Lionel Atwill) threatens an investigator with a gorilla brain transplant – are its only real highlights.

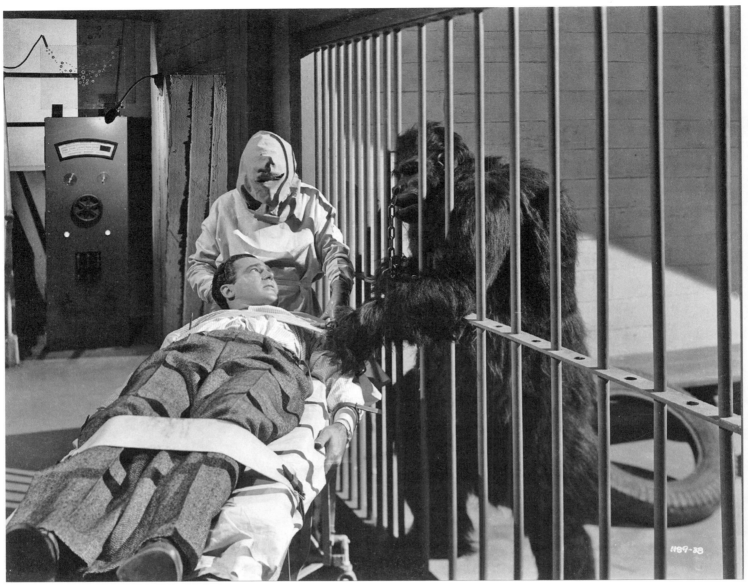

THE STRANGE CASE OF DR. RX – PRODUCTION
PHOTOGRAPH (*ABOVE*); PUBLICITY PHOTOGRAPH (*OPPOSITE PAGE*).
"AMOUR" – PHOTOGRAPHIC ART BY WILLIAM MORTENSEN (*RIGHT*).

1. Ray Corrigan also appears to be the man in the ape-suit featured in "Amour", a notorious photographic construct by William Mortensen, in which a huge gorilla is shown slavering over a half-naked woman with blood streaming from her mouth. If the generally-attributed creation date of mid-1930s for "Amour" is correct, Corrigan later recreated the image in a set of less explicit publicity photographs for **The Strange Case Of Dr. RX** – although the reverse seems more likely.

1189-35AD

MR. WASHINGTON GOES TO TOWN
(Jed Buell, 1940: USA)
One of the last memorable film "coons" was Mantan Moreland, whose jittery
comedic character featured in a huge array of movies in the late 30s and 40s; a typical
example is Jean Yarbrough horror-comedy **King Of The Zombies** (1941), with a plot
which fuses a mad doctor, foreign spies and the living dead with the continual
comedic commentary of Moreland, who plays a superstitious manservant highly
attuned – like most coon stereotypes – to the supernatural. This primitive fear is at
the heart of the all-black **Mr. Washington Goes To Town**, in which Moreland and
his regular accomplice F.E. Miller play a pair of jailed convicts, one of whom
(Moreland) learns he has inherited a hotel. He subsequently has a bizarre nightmare
about this establishment, which takes up the bulk of the film. In his dream, the hotel
is populated by a range of human and animal oddities, including a huge gorilla
(played by ape impersonator Clarence Morehouse). **Mr. Washington Goes To Town**
was produced by Jed Buell and Ted Toddy's Dixie National Pictures; another horror-
tinged farce from that team was the "mad doctor" movie **Professor Creeps** (1942),
which ends as Mantan and Miller, playing a pair of coon detectives, are turned into
animals and encounter a crazed gorilla (a role latterly accredited to Emil Van Horn).
Moreland was teamed with yet another gorilla (again played by Emil van Horn) in
Jean Yarbrough's **Law Of The Jungle** (1942) – a Monogram mess about Nazi
agitators in war-time Africa.

LAW OF THE JUNGLE – WITH EMIL VAN HORN AS GORILLA;
PRODUCTION PHOTOGRAPHS.

SON OF INGAGI
(Richard C. Kahn, 1940: USA)

An insane female scientist keeps a hairy ape-man in a cage until it escapes and drinks poison. Completely unrelated to the 1930 gorilla-sex movie **Ingagi**, Kahn's film simply borrowed its title to generate interest. An extremely low-budget effort from race-film company Hollywood Productions, **Son Of Ingagi** was, if possible, even stranger than its namesake, and is mostly notable for being a rare all-black "horror" movie (one thankfully lacking in any form of comic relief). It was scripted by Spencer Williams Jr., better-known as a director of "fire-and-brimstone" religious fables.

JUNGLE GIRL
(William Witney & John English, 1941: USA)

Officially based on the 1931 pulp novel *Jungle Girl* by Edgar Rice Burroughs, but actually substantially different, **Jungle Girl** was a classic Republic serial, blending jungle adventure iconography (including Emil Van Horn in a weird gorilla costume) with sex appeal (short-skirted actress Frances Gifford as Nyoka, the girl of the title) and a series of sado-masochistic scenarios in which Gifford appears in a life-threatening situation, usually in bondage. These scenes include Nyoka trapped in a

JUNGLE GIRL
1096-EP-10-9

blazing oil swamp, Nyoka bound to an altar as a human sacrifice, and Nyoka trapped in a tomb of poison gas. **Jungle Girl**'s fifteen chapters were: **Death By Voodoo, Queen Of Beasts, River Of Fire, Treachery, Jungle Vengeance, Tribal Fury, The Poison Dart, Man Trap, Treasure Tomb, Jungle Killer, Dangerous Secret, Trapped, Ambush, Diamond Trail,** and **Flight To Freedom.** Nyoka reappeared in 1942 in a sequel serial, **Perils Of Nyoka** (later condensed into the feature **Nyoka And The Tigermen**), with the action (including more bondage and light torture) transposed to an equally race-hateful desert setting.[1] Nyoka was now played by Kay Aldridge, and the cast again included ape-specialist Emil Van Horn – this time as Satan, the savage gorilla-guard of the sadistic Queen Vultura, played by Lorna Gray. Nyoka's many perils include a huge, Poe-style swinging pendulum-blade and a ceiling of descending spikes. Stuntgirl Helen Thurston featured heavily as a body double in both serials. In an inversion from the usual process of film producers licensing comic characters, Fawcett Comics decided to launch a comic based on Republic's Nyoka character; after a one-off *Jungle Girl* issue in 1942, the first issue of *Nyoka The Jungle Girl* was published in 1945, and the comic ran until 1953. The first "jungle girl" comic character was Will Eisner's Sheena, created in 1937, whose own comic *Sheena, Queen Of The Jungle* also debuted in 1942, running for 18 issues.[3] It was preceded by *Fantomah, Mystery Woman Of the Jungle*, which debuted in 1940, as did Marga, the Panther Woman, a vicious female fighter raised by big jungle cats, who appeared in *Science Comics*. Kara, Jungle Princess appeared in *Exciting Comics* in 1945, followed by Princess Pantha (in *Thrilling Comics*, 1946), *Rulah, Jungle Goddess* (in Zoot Comics, 1947), and *Tegra, Jungle Empress* – which changed to *Zegra, Jungle Empress* with issue #2 – in 1948. These comics and the concurrent glut of 1940s jungle girl movies and serials doubtlessly fed each other's popularity in a symbiosis which continued into the early 50s. The jungle girl pulp fever even spread to Italy, where Gian Giacomo Dalmasso and Enzo Magni's *Pantera Bionda* ("Blonde Panther") was one of the initial wave of post-war *fumetti*, first appearing in April 1948; sadly, Pantera Bionda's skimpy costume soon came under fire from censors and religious maniacs, forcing the artist to make changes which in turn doomed his *fumetto* to extinction in 1950. It remains a key publication in the history of Italian erotic comics.

1. **Perils Of Nyoka**'s fifteen chapters, all with two-word titles, were: **Desert Intrigue, Death's Chariot, Devil's Crucible, Ascending Doom, Fatal Second, Human Sacrifice, Monster's Clutch, Tuareg Vengeance, Burned Alive, Treacherous Trail, Unknown Peril, Underground Tornado, Thundering Death, Blazing Barrier,** and **Satan's Fury.** Footage from **Jungle Girl** was recycled in Republic's notoriously cheap feature **Daughter Of The Jungle** (1948), which starred Lois Hall as Ticoora, a white jungle queen, as well as in their penultimate serial, **Panther Girl Of The Kongo** (1955), a jungle horror with a mad scientist who creates a mutant breed of giant "claw monsters".

THE PERILS OF NYOKA – PRODUCTION PHOTOGRAPH.

THE MONSTER AND THE GIRL – PRODUCTION
PHOTOGRAPHS.

The MONSTER AND THE GIRL
(Stuart Heisler, 1941: USA)
Filmed as **Dead On Arrival**, and originally rejected for the PCA on grounds of
depicting white slavery, **The Monster And The Girl** was the latest in a long line of
"gorilla" movies, featuring a man-to-ape brain transplant. A girl tricked into
prostitution, a young man framed and executed for murder, ruthless gangsters,
surgical experiments by a mad doctor (played by George Zucco), and a gorilla on a
homicidal revenge-spree are the basic components of this hybrid offering – half sleazy
crime thriller, half trash-horror – from Paramount. The killer ape was played
(uncredited) by Charles Gemora, in a markedly more realistic costume than his earlier
creations.

KEEP 'EM FLYING
(Arthur Lubin, 1941: USA)
Emil Van Horn is the gorilla-man in this otherwise forgettable Abbot and Costello comedy feature. one of the many such roles he played during the early 1940s. The comic duo would team up with another famous gorilla man, Charles Gemora, in **Africa Screams** (1949).

DR. RENAULT'S SECRET – PRODUCTION PHOTOGRAPH.

DR. RENAULT'S SECRET
(Harry Lachman, 1942: USA)
The third direct film adaptation of Gaston Leroux's novel *Balaoo*, a story of evolutionary genetics taken to transgressive extremes. **Dr. Renault's Secret** featured several actors familiar from low-budget horror movies, including George Zucco as the mad scientist, Renault, and J. Carrol Naish as his human-ape hybrid. Stuntman Ray Corrigan, one of several ape impersonators active during the 1930s and 1940s, appears in costume as a gorilla. The film reportedly ran into censorship issues relating to religion (Darwin's theory of evolution was still offensive to the more simple-minded) and "gruesomeness". Ultimately, Naish's harmless-looking creature cannot compare to the truly grotesque human beast from **The Wizard,** the definitive 1927 rendering of Leroux's grisly fable.

THE APE MAN – PRODUCTION PHOTOGRAPHS.

The APE MAN
(William Beaudine, 1943: USA)
One of the string of low-budget Monogram horror movies made by Bela Lugosi in the 40s; here he plays a mad scientist who turns himself into a feral hybrid by injecting an ape's spinal fluid. Needing human spinal fluid to reverse the process, logically, he sends out his pet gorilla (played by Emil Van Horn) to kill – a slightly variant reprise of Monogram's **The Ape** from 1940. **Return Of The Ape Man** (1944) was an unrelated film about cryogenic experimentation, which leads two scientists (Lugosi again, plus John Carradine) to revive a long-frozen prehistoric man. Despite a one-hemisphere brain transplant, the brute goes on a homicidal rampage. That was Lugosi's last horror role for Monogram.

CAPTIVE WILD WOMAN – PRODUCTION PHOTOGRAPHS (*ABOVE & OPPOSITE TOP*).

JUNGLE CAPTIVE – PRODUCTION PHOTOGRAPH (*OPPOSITE BOTTOM*).

CAPTIVE WILD WOMAN

(Edward Dmytryk, 1943: USA)

Deriving from human medical experimentation and grafting films such as Erle C Kenton's seminal **Island Of Lost Souls**, this is the tale of a doctor (John Carradine) who turns an ape, Cheela (played by Ray "Crash" Corrigan) into a semi-human female through gland and brain transplanting. Finally she is given fully human form, but reverts to bestiality when aroused. The mysterious Acquanetta plays the she-creature. The film's low budget meant that director Dmytryk was forced to use extensive stock circus footage, which was culled from a previous Universal production, **The Big Cage** (1933). **Captive Wild Woman** spawned two sequels: **Jungle Woman** (1944) and **Jungle Captive** (1945, with facially deformed actor Rondo Hatton). Acquanetta returned for **Jungle Woman**, but was replaced by starlet Vicky Lane in the third movie, which also recycled footage from **Captive Wild Woman**.

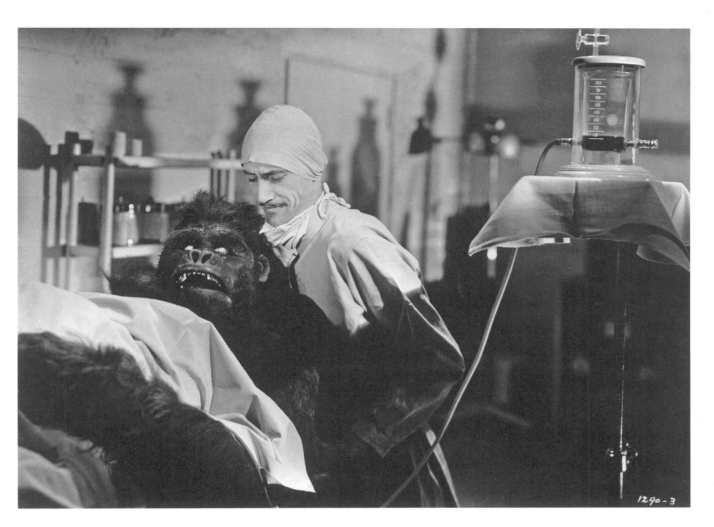

DIZZY DETECTIVES – PRODUCTION PHOTOGRAPH (*ABOVE*).
A BIRD IN THE HEAD – PRODUCTION PHOTOGRAPH
(*OPPOSITE TOP*); CRIME ON THEIR HANDS – PRODUCTION
PHOTOGRAPH (*OPPOSITE BOTTOM*).

DIZZY DETECTIVES

(Jules White, 1943: USA)

The decade's most prolific purveyors of comic horror may have been the Three Stooges, with a series of short subjects which blended their brand of trash idiocy with generic fright-film iconography. In **Dizzy Detectives** (1943), the trio play policemen who investigate a series of robberies which appear to have been perpetrated by a monster gorilla, a classic old dark house denizen; Ray Corrigan plays the burglar-gorilla. Other Three Stooges filmd with horror elements include **Spook Louder** (1943, with Japanese spies dressed as ghouls and a death-ray),[1] **Idle Roomers** (1944), with screen heavy Duke York as a wolf-man, **Three Pests In A Mess** (1945, with ghouls in a graveyard), and **A Bird In The Head** (1946), in which Art Miles again featured as a gorilla detailed for a human brain transplant. Another gorilla (Steve Calvert) appeared in **Crime On Their Hands** (1948), while **Shivering Sherlocks** (also 1948) featured Duke York as a rampaging hunchback with an axe. **Who Done It?** (1949) was a remake of Del Lord's **You're Next!**, with Duke York as a monstrous "goon" in a sinister mansion.

1. A remake of Del Lord's 1933 **The Great Pie Mystery**, produced by Mack Sennett.

© D·4111·12

The MONSTER MAKER
(Sam Newfield, 1944: USA)

From PRC, this film was another in the prolific horror sub-genre of human medical experiments which flourished in the 1940s. In **The Monster Maker**, a Slavic scientist named Markoff infects a man with a serum which causes acromegaly, the progressively disfiguring pituitary syndrome, in order to blackmail him into surrendering his daughter in marriage. We also learn that Markoff previously infected his wife in a similar way, so that she would be too ugly for other men; as a result, she killed herself. Played by J. Carroll Naish, Markoff is drawn as a Sadean beast who sees others as sub-human pawns to be used, abused or disposed of at will. Commendable for this depiction of absolute evil, the film is also remarkable for the special effects make-up used on the acromegaly victim, which was seemingly directly modelled on the cranio-facial deformities of Joseph "John" Merrick, the English show-freak known as the Elephant Man. Ray "Crash" Corrigan makes one of his numerous appearances in gorilla costume, and Glenn Strange plays Markoff's giant assistant. **The Monster Maker** was the latest addition to a shadowy cinematic sub-genre which, knowingly or not, reflected in its lurid plotlines the hideous medical experiments which were simultaneously being performed on helpless prisoners in Germany's Nazi death camps; in this case, the SS program of deliberate infection with deadly diseases which was carried out at Dachau, Mauthausen, Buchenwald, Neuengamme, Ravensbrück, Sachsenhausen and Auschwitz.

GILDERSLEEVE'S GHOST
(Gordon Douglas, 1944: USA)
This haunted house farce with an invisible woman, mad scientist, ghosts and a gorilla was one of the numerous films in which Charles Gemora appeared, uncredited, during the 1940s.

GILDERSLEEVE'S GHOST – PRODUCTION PHOTOGRAPH.

NABONGA GORILLA – PRODUCTION PHOTOGRAPHS.

NABONGA GORILLA

(Sam Newfield, 1944: USA)

Poverty row's favourite tropes of stock-footage jungle mayhem and men in ape-suits menacing scantily-clad girls achieved a delirious fusion in the mid-1940s with the release of three monochrome films starring Ray "Crash" Corrigan – **Nabonga Gorilla** (filmed as **Jungle Terror**), **White Pongo**, and **The White Gorilla**. With Corrigan in costume as Samson, a homicidal gorilla, 18-year-old Julie London as the ape's jungle-girl mistress, and Buster Crabbe as the hero, PRC's **Nabonga Gorilla** starts slowly but hots up when all the parties concerned – including a male and female villain – converge on a hidden jungle zone at whose epicentre lies a plane wreck housing the skull of a dead aviator, and the cave where the sexually ripe girl and her feral guardian live with a chest of stolen treasures. All the highlights belong to Samson, who is briefly caged but later smashes to death the two screaming looters; his violent reaction when the hero touches his mistress is suggestive of sexual jealousy, adding a vague notion of bestiality to the proceedings. Corrigan was actually credited as Nbongo, seemingly to imply that the role was played by a real gorilla. The same director supervised **White Pongo** (1945), produced by his brother Sigmund Neufeld for PRC, for which Corrigan created a new, stunning white ape-suit in order to portray an albino gorilla (although he would receive no cast credit). Highlights of the jungle-

hunt for White Pongo – said to be an unusually intelligent "missing link" between man and monkeys – are some primal scenes of native rituals, ghostly nocturnal shots of the white ape in its habitat, some screaming smash-deaths, and a climactic battle between white and black gorilla over the prone body of a human female. In the end, White Pongo is shot and wounded, caged, and shipped back to civilization and a future of anthropological exhibition. Both **Nabonga** and **White Pongo** utilize quantities of stock footage, but both pale besides **The White Gorilla** (1945), the kind of found-footage collage-film usually only created in the bowels of exploitation cinema. Nominally directed by H.L. Fraser, and seemingly conceived purely to get more mileage out of Corrigan's white ape-suit, **The White Gorilla** is primarily constructed from chunks of the silent serial **The Perils Of The Jungle** (1927), written by Fraser. Corrigan was drafted in for the shooting of new footage, in which he appears both as a human and as the titular albino gorilla (named Konga), and to provide a voice-over narration which attempts to weld the two visual strands, markedly different in both film-stock and running-speed. The project was supervised by Louis Weiss, who would also be involved in the tits-and-octopus travesty **Devil Monster** not long afterwards. Corrigan impersonated a slightly different creature – a giant sloth-monkey hybrid – in **Unknown Island** (1948), a Cinecolor dinosaur movie in which the upright-walking tyrannosaurs were played by men in rubber suits,

WHITE GORILLA – PRODUCTION PHOTOGRAPHS (*THIS PAGE*).
WHITE PONGO – PRODUCTION PHOTOGRAPH (*OPPOSITE PAGE*).

TALL DARK AND GRUESOME – PRODUCTION PHOTOGRAPH (*OVERLEAF VERSO TOP*); MICROSPOOK – PRODUCTION PHOTOGRAPH (*OVERLEAF VERSO BOTTOM*).
THE LOST TRIBE – PRODUCTION PHOTOGRAPH (*OVERLEAF RECTO TOP*); MARK OF THE GORILLA – PRODUCTION PHOTOGRAPHS (*OVERLEAF RECTO BOTTOM*).

prefiguring the more celebrated use of this effect in Japanese company Toho's *kaiju* ("strange monster") movies of the 1950s. Corrigan's final appearance as a gorilla may have been in **The Lost Tribe**, shot in 1948, the first in a Sam Katzman-produced series of films based on the comic-strip adventurer Jungle Jim (played by former Tarzan Johnny Weissmuller); Corrigan's suit certainly features (as an ape named Zimba who leads other gorillas in a mass attack), but it may not be Corrigan inside – at some point in 1948 he reportedly sold most of his suits to stunt extra Steve Calvert and decided to retire from ape impersonation. Among Calvert's first roles were a crazed gorilla in the Del Lord horror-comedy **Tall, Dark And Gruesome** (1948), and the titular giant ape in **Zamba** (1949), who raises a small white boy stranded in the jungle (the Corrigan suit also appeared, briefly and uncredited, in the short Harry Von Zell prank-film **Microspook**, again made in 1949). Shot the same year but released early in 1950 were two more low-budget jungle romps with ape-suit antics – Jack Schwarz Productions' **Forbidden Jungle**, which rivals **The White Gorilla** in its blend of repetitive stock footage and lunatic narrative, and Columbia's **Mark Of The Gorilla**, another adventure for Jungle Jim who must battle murderous, treasure-hunting Nazis dressed as gorillas (Calvert's first accredited ape-suit role).

SPOOK BUSTERS
(William Beaudine, 1946: USA)

In 1939 producer Sam Katzman signed up a number of louts-turned-actors, formerly known as the Dead End Kids, and renamed them the East Side Kids, which is how they are billed in the two Monogram "horror-comedies" **Spooks Run Wild** (1941) and **Ghosts On The Loose** (1943), both with Bela Lugosi. In 1946 the East Side Kids morphed again, becoming the Bowery Boys; one of their first film vehicles was another Monogram horror-comedy, **Spook Busters**, which relies for laughs on one of the oldest fright-movie clichés, a human-gorilla brain transplant by a mad doctor in a haunted house. The gorilla was played by Art Miles, an ape-impersonator whose costume was especially grotesque; Miles had earlier played a gorilla in Katzman's **Crazy Knights** (1944), yet another haunted house spoof. Filmed under the working title **Ghost Busters**, **Spook Busters** largely borrows its establishing premise from the equally anodyne 1937 Mickey Mouse cartoon **Lonesome Ghosts**.

CRAZY KNIGHTS – PRODUCTION PHOTOGRAPH.

CONGO BILL

(Spencer Gordon Bennet, 1948: USA)

Based on a 1940 DC Comics character, Columbia's 15-chapter **Congo Bill** was the last jungle serial of the decade. Like many other such narratives, it revolved around the popular trope of a white-skinned ruler of African savages. The serial's chapters were: **The Untamed Beast; Jungle Gold; A Hot Reception; Congo Bill Springs A Trap; White Shadows In The Jungle; The White Queen; Black Panther; Sinister Schemes; The Witch Doctor Strikes; Trail Of Treachery; A Desperate Chance; The Lair Of The Beast; Menace Of The Jungle; Treasure Map;** and **The Missing Letter**. It included provocative scenes of a flimsily-attired blonde menaced by a rapist-gorilla, a monster which also threatens to kill human males in several sequences. Either Ray Corrigan or Steve Calvert is thought to be the man in the ape-costume.

CONGO BILL – PRODUCTION PHOTOGRAPH (*FOLLOWING PAGES*).

The MONSTER AND THE APE
(Howard Bretherton, 1945: USA)
After several years in the wilderness, serials returned to the pulp SF genre with this 15-chapter Columbia release, seemingly inspired by Republic's earlier **The Mysterious Doctor Satan**. An inventor creates a monstrous robot, named Metalogen Man, only to have it stolen by an evil scientist and his trained ape, Thor (played by Ray "Crash" Corrigan). The serial's fifteen chapters were: **The Mechanical Terror; The Edge Of Doom; Flames Of Fate; The Fatal Search; Rocks Of Doom; A Friend In Disguise; A Scream In The Night; Death In The Dark; The Secret Tunnel; Forty Thousand Volts; The Mad Professor; Shadows Of Destiny; The Gorilla At Large; His Last Flight;** and **Justice Triumphs**. Lacking the quality of many of its competitors, **The Monster And The Ape** nonetheless indicated a growing public appetite for science fiction in the immediate post-war period; this was reflected in the production of such SF-oriented serials as **The Purple Monster Strikes** (Republic, 1945), **The Crimson Ghost** (Republic, 1946), **The Mysterious Mr. M** (1946 – Universal's final film serial), and **King Of The Rocket Men** (Republic, 1949).

WHO KILLED DOC ROBBIN?
(Bernard Carr, 1948: USA)
Hal Roach belatedly returned to the gang-of-kids-in-haunted-house-with-gorilla format with this over-long attempt to being back the glory days of **Our Gang**. Charles Gemora is also said to have returned to play the monster ape, making it among his final such roles.

WHO KILLED DOC ROBBIN? – PRODUCTION PHOTOGRAPH.

MIGHTY JOE YOUNG – PRODUCTION PHOTOGRAPH.

MIGHTY JOE YOUNG
(Ernest B. Schoedsack, 1949: USA)
Directed by Schoedsack form an original story by his **King Kong** co-creator Merian
C. Cooper, **Mighty Joe Young** was the pair's last cinematic foray into the world of
giant apes. Willis O'Brien again provided animation for the gorilla, reportedly aided
by a young apprentice named Ray Harryhausen. While the film's plot is essentially a
more youth-oriented echo of **Kong** – giant ape is taken from the wild by a promoter
and condemned to a life in chains in the name of entertainment – **Mighty Joe Young**
remains a fitting end to Hollywood's age of black-and-white fantasy cinema.

INDEX of FILMS

INDEX of FILMS

Gareth Hugh Janus is editor of numerous books on pulp cinema and pulp art. His main project is the popular book series **VOLUPTUOUS TERRORS**, an ongoing collection showcasing classic Italian horror and exploitation film posters of the 1950s to 1980s.

VOLUPTUOUS TERRORS – THE SERIES TO DATE

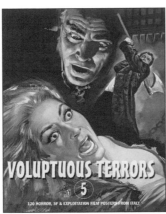  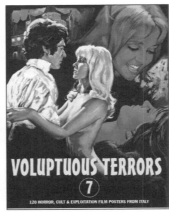 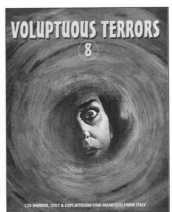

SHADOWS IN A PHANTOM EYE – THE SERIES TO DATE

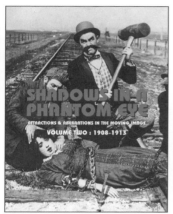

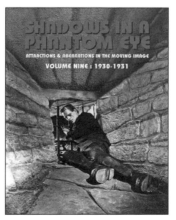